Gary E. McCuen

IDEAS IN CONFLICT SERIES

502 Second Street
Hudson, Wisconsin 54016
phone (715) 386-7113

Library of Congress Cataloging-in-Publication Data

Illiteracy in America.

    (Ideas in conflict)
    Bibliography: p.
    Summary: A collection of essays presenting a variety
of, often conflicting viewpoints concerning the problem
of illiteracy and what can be done about it.
    1. Literacy—United States. [1. Literacy] I. McCuen,
Gary E. II. Series.
LC151.143 1988   374'.012   87-91951
ISBN 0-86596-067-4

Illustration & photo credits

Bruce Beattie 19, Carnegie Foundation for the Advancement of Teaching 118, The Guardian 23, Charles Keller 143, Doug MacGregor 42, Jeff MacNelly 58, The National Commission on Excellence in Education 112, The National Advisory Council on Adult Education 80, Office of Educational Research and Improvement (U.S. Department of Education) 97, Bill Sanders 36, Sam Scrawls 65, David Seavey 48, 119, 126, Steve Skelley 105, U.S. Department of Education 72, U.S. House of Representatives Committee on Education and Labor 59.

© 1988 by Gary E. McCuen Publications, Inc.
502 Second Street • Hudson, Wisconsin 54016
    (715) 386-7113
International Standard Book Number 0-86596-067-4
Printed in the United States of America

CONTENTS

CHAPTER 3 THE SOCIAL FOUNDATIONS
OF EDUCATIONAL FAILURE

REASONING SKILL DEVELOPMENT

These activities may be used as individualized study guides for students in libraries and resource centers or as discussion catalysts in small group and classroom discussions.

IDEAS in CONFLICT ®

This series features ideas in conflict on political, social, and moral issues. It presents counterpoints, debates, opinions, commentary, and analysis for use in libraries and classrooms. Each title in the series uses one or more of the following basic elements:

Introductions *that present an issue overview giving historic background and/or a description of the controversy.*

Counterpoints *and debates carefully chosen from publications, books, and position papers on the political right and left to help librarians and teachers respond to requests that treatment of public issues be fair and balanced.*

Symposiums *and forums that go beyond debates that can polarize and oversimplify. These present commentary from across the political spectrum that reflect how complex issues attract many shades of opinion.*

A **global** *emphasis with foreign perspectives and surveys on various moral questions and political issues that will help readers to place subject matter in a less culture-bound and ethnocentric frame of reference. In an ever-shrinking and interdependent world, understanding and cooperation are essential. Many issues are global in nature and can be effectively dealt with only by common efforts and international understanding.*

Reasoning skill *study guides and discussion activities provide ready-made tools for helping with critical reading and evaluation of content. The guides and activities deal with one or more of the following:*

RECOGNIZING AUTHOR'S POINT OF VIEW

INTERPRETING EDITORIAL CARTOONS

VALUES IN CONFLICT

WHAT IS EDITORIAL BIAS?
WHAT IS SEX BIAS?
WHAT IS POLITICAL BIAS?
WHAT IS ETHNOCENTRIC BIAS?
WHAT IS RACE BIAS?
WHAT IS RELIGIOUS BIAS?

*From across **the political spectrum** varied sources are presented for research projects and classroom discussions. Diverse opinions in the series come from magazines, newspapers, syndicated columnists, books, political speeches, foreign nations, and position papers by corporations and nonprofit institutions.*

About the Editor

Gary E. McCuen is an editor and publisher of anthologies for public libraries and curriculum materials for schools. Over the past 17 years his publications of over 200 titles have specialized in social, moral, and political conflict. They include books, pamphlets, cassettes, tabloids, filmstrips, and simulation games, many of them designed from his curriculums during 11 years of teaching junior and senior high school social studies. At present he is the editor and publisher of the *Ideas in Conflict* series and the *Editorial Forum* series.

CHAPTER 1

THE ILLITERACY PROBLEM

1 THE ILLITERACY PROBLEM

THE ILLITERACY RATE IS A SOURCE OF NATIONAL PRIDE

National Assessment of Educational Progress

The National Assessment of Educational Progress (NAEP) is funded by the Office for Educational Research and Improvement under a grant to Educational Testing Service. National Assessment is an education research project mandated by Congress to collect data over time on the performance of young Americans in various learning areas. It makes available information on assessment procedures to state and local education agencies.

Points to Consider:

1. Why do the authors of the report tell us to celebrate Literate America?
2. How does the NAEP define literacy?
3. What group of people performed significantly better on the NAEP reading scale and why?
4. Explain the NAEP's conclusion that "illiteracy" is not a major problem but "literacy" is a problem.
5. What percentage of young adults are estimated to read as well as or better than the average eighth-grade student?

Irwin S. Kirsch and Ann Jungeblut, *Literacy: Profiles of America's Young Adults, Final Report* (Report No. 16-PL-01). Princeton, N.J.: National Assessment of Educational Progress, 1986.

Although some of our citizens reach adulthood unable to read and write, we are a better educated and more literate society than at any time in our history.

Is illiteracy a major problem among young adults in the United States?

That is the major question addressed by the work summarized in this report: work that has produced the most conceptually and analytically sophisticated study of adult literacy ever conducted in this country. Now we, as readers, may judge for ourselves what the answer to the question must be.

Conceptually, this study avoids the almost universal tendency to oversimplify the nature of literacy and to divide the population into neat categories of "illiterate," "functionally illiterate," and "literate." Rather, it recognizes that people develop a variety of literacy abilities that reflect the social settings in which they interact with printed materials, whether this be the home, community, school, or workplace. The investigators in this study have produced a "profile of adult literacy" that provides four perspectives on how well young adults aged 21 through 25 years perform literacy tasks involving the use of prose materials (which predominate in home and school settings), documents (like forms, procedural guides, manuals, and so forth that are widely used in commercial and civil life in the United States), quantitative literacy materials (in which reading and mathematics are intertwined, as in reading a menu and calculating the cost of a meal), and materials used by fourth, eighth, and eleventh grade students in school.

Literate America

Analyses in this report reveal that, based on the standard of "literacy" of a hundred years ago, the ability to sign one's name, virtually all young adults are "literate." If the standard of the World War II era, some 50 years ago is applied, almost 95 percent of young adults are estimated to meet or exceed the performance of fourth grade students. Based on the standard of the War on Poverty, twenty-five years ago, 80 percent of young adults meet or exceed the performance of students in the eighth grade. . . .

So here we are. On the one hand we should, as a nation, celebrate Literate America, for the last century has witnessed the remarkable feat of bringing more than 95 percent of young adults to levels of literacy that exceed by far the results of the mass literacy campaigns of the Soviet Union and Cuba, in which illiteracy was declared to have been "eradicated" when the adult population reached third grade levels of achievement. By the standards of international mass literacy campaigns, the United States is a nation of literates.

CAN JOHNNY READ?

The often heard charge, "Johnny can't read," is a little like saying "Johnny can't cook." Johnny may be able to read the directions for constructing a radio kit, but not a Henry James novel, just as Johnny may be able to fry an egg but not cook Peking duck. In discussing reading in schools, we must recognize that reading involves as wide a range of different types of texts as there are types of food. And, to imply, as does the slogan "Johnny can't read," that reading is a single skill suited to all types of texts does not do justice to the range of reading types.

Beach and Appleman in Becoming Readers in a Complex Society, *1984*

Improvement Necessary

Yet, by the standards of the information age, we should press harder for more rigorous education and training in the knowledge and information processing skills that now limit the flexibility of the 50 percent or so of our adults who possess "mid-level" literacy. As the need emerges to engage more often in retraining and continuing education in the face of change, lack of the skill to learn rapidly from textual materials in concentrated programs or in on-the-job learning sessions will strain the capabilities of the "mid-level" literates. What we need now are education and training programs that can develop the existing literacy skills of adults to higher levels while providing the knowledge to master the new challenges that will face today's young adults in the twenty-first century. . . .

Today, the information processing requirements associated with the broad range of materials and purposes people have for reading require that our nation's focus on literacy shift from one of "How many," to one recognizing the various types and levels of literacy characteristic of our society today. No longer can we rely on distinctions based on the simplistic notion that "literates" and "illiterates" can be neatly pigeonholed . . . .

Literacy Defined

In order to take account of the many points of view that exist regarding literacy, the National Assessment of Educational Progress (NAEP) convened panels of experts who helped set the framework for this assessment. Their deliberations led to the definition of literacy adopted:

11

Using printed and written information to function in society, to achieve one's goals, and to develop one's knowledge and potential....

NAEP characterized the literacy skills of America's young adults in terms of three "literacy scales" representing distinct and important aspects of literacy:

■ prose literacy—the knowledge and skills needed to understand and use information from texts that include editorials, news stories, poems, and the like;

■ document literacy—the knowledge and skills required to locate and use information contained in job applications or payroll forms, bus schedules, maps, tables, indexes, and so forth; and,

■ quantitative literacy—the knowledge and skills needed to apply arithmetic operations, either alone or sequentially, that are embedded in printed materials, such as in balancing a checkbook, figuring out a tip, completing an order form, or determining the amount of interest from a loan advertisement.

Major Findings

► The literacy problem identified for the nation's young adults can be characterized in two ways: While the overwhelming majority of young adults adequately perform tasks at the lower levels on each of the three scales, sizable numbers appear unable to do well on tasks of moderate complexity. Only a relatively small percentage of this group is estimated to perform at levels typified by the more complex and challenging tasks.

► Inevitably, smaller percentages of young adults are found to perform at increasing levels of proficiency on each of the scales. The fact that fewer and fewer individuals attain these moderate and high levels of proficiency is most pronounced for young adults who terminate their education early and for minority group members.

► Black young adults, on average, perform significantly below white young adults—by almost a full standard deviation. Hispanic young adults, on average, perform about midway between their black and white peers. These differences appear at each level of education reported.

► Nearly half of the white and Hispanic young adults who enrolled in a GED (General Educational Development) program went on to attain the credential, compared with less than one-fourth of the black young adults.

► Home-support variables (such as parents' education and access to literacy materials) were found to be significantly related to the type and amount of education and to the literacy practices reported by young adults. These, in turn, help to explain differences in literacy-skill levels.

► On average, young adults perform significantly better on the NAEP reading scale than do in-school 17-year-olds. This suggests that further education and participation in society contribute to the improvement of reading skills represented by that scale.

► Only about two percent of this young-adult population were estimated to have such limited literacy skills that it was judged that the simulation tasks would unduly frustrate or embarrass them. Roughly one percent (or about half) of this group reported being unable to speak English.

► The English-speaking one percent, instead of attempting the simulation tasks, responded to a set of oral-language tasks. The comparatively low performance indicates that this group (about 225,000 people) may have a language problem that extends beyond processing printed information.

Major Conclusions

► It is clear from these data that "illiteracy" is not a major problem for this population. It is also clear, however, that "literacy" is a problem. Sizable numbers of individuals are estimated to perform within the middle range on each of the scales. Within these broad ranges, individuals are neither totally "illiterate" nor fully "literate" for a technologically advanced society.

► The overwhelming majority of America's young adults are able to use printed information to accomplish many tasks that are either routine or uncomplicated. It is distressing, however, that relatively small proportions of young adults are estimated to be proficient at levels characterized by the more moderate or relatively complex tasks. It has been argued that many, if not most, of society's managerial, professional, and technical service-sector jobs will require participation in some postsecondary program. This argument raises the question of whether or not individuals with more limited literacy skills will qualify for or benefit from such education and training programs.

► As a society, we will have to develop and apply appropriate intervention strategies to meet the diverse needs of these young adults. Strategies must be tailored not only to help those whose literacy skills are most limited, but also to upgrade the literacy skills of those who demonstrate low to moderate levels of proficiencies. In addition, we must find ways to expand the number of those in our population who are able to perform society's more challenging tasks.

► The relatively poor performance of minority group members and those who terminated their education early, combined with the projected changes in demographics for the 21-to 25-year-old population, suggest that unless we develop and implement more appropriate intervention and prevention strategies, America will have a less literate pool of young adults to fill its human resource needs over the next decade or so.

► To the extent that the skills identified in this literacy study are important for full participation in our society, this assessment raises questions about whether we should seek better ways to teach the current curriculum or whether we need to reconsider what is taught as well as how we teach it.

► It is clear that there is no single step or simple action, which if taken, will allow all individuals to become fully literate. Becoming literate in our society is a lifelong pursuit affected by such factors as home environment, economic situation, aspirations, opportunities, and education. As a result, we must recognize the intergenerational effects on literacy. . . .

A More Literate Society

Characterizing America as an "illiterate nation" is a little like characterizing America as a "diseased nation." Although millions suffer each year from debilitating illnesses, as a nation we are living longer and healthier lives than ever before. Similarly, although some of our citizens reach adulthood unable to read and write, we are a better educated and more literate society than at any time in our history.

Indeed NAEP's assessment of the literacy skills and strategies of young adults ages 21 to 25 years clearly indicates that the vast majority are literate according to standards applied by some scholars and historians. Virtually all young adults today demonstrate the ability to sign their name, thus making them literate according to standards applied to information available more than 100 years ago. Roughly 95 percent of the young adults reach or surpass the level of reading typical of the average fourth grader—the fourth grade being the standard adopted by the military almost half a century ago. By more recent standards, 80 percent of young adults are estimated to read as well as or better than the average eighth-grade student and more than 60 percent are estimated to read as well or better than the average eleventh-grade student. . . .

Important Issues

To the extent that the skills identified in this literacy assessment are important for full participation in our society, this study raises some important issues. Should we seek better ways to teach the current curriculum or do we need to reconsider what is taught and how we teach it? Adult literacy programs aimed at developing comprehension skills are frequently based on elementary school reading models that, for the most part, are restricted to the use of narrative texts. Results from this and other studies suggest that primary emphases on a single aspect of literacy may not lead to the acquisition of the complex information-processing skills and strategies needed to cope successfully with the broad array of tasks adults face.

Other adult literacy programs that tend to focus on the acquisition of skills associated with discrete tasks, such as filling out a job application form or using a bus schedule, may have limited impact for the individual. This may be so because, while literacy is not a single skill suited to all types of texts, neither is it an infinite number of isolated skills each associated with a given type of text or document. Rather, as this assessment shows, there may be an ordered set of information-processing skills and strategies that may be called into play to accomplish the range of tasks represented in the various aspects of literacy as defined here.

As one final point, becoming fully literate in a technologically advanced society is a lifelong pursuit, as is sustaining good health. Both are complex and depend upon a number of factors. So, just as there is no single action or step, that if taken, will ensure the physical health of every individual, there is no single action or step, that if taken, will ensure that every individual will become fully literate.

THE ILLITERACY PROBLEM

THERE IS LITTLE TO CELEBRATE

Jonathan Kozol

Jonathan Kozol is the author of Illiterate America. *This reading is adapted from a report that was presented to the American Society of Newspaper Editors and the American Newspaper Publishers Association.*

Points to Consider:

1. What percentage of American citizens can read and write?
2. Why did the authors of the Princeton study advise the press to "celebrate" the study's findings?
3. What is the percentage of adults that cannot make use of a road map?
4. How has illiteracy affected other areas of American society?

Not by "yesterday's standards" but today's, not by Third World standards but American criteria, readers competent to understand the written press and find enjoyment in simple verse are an endangered species.

Education writers do not have an enviable job these days. Every month, a new statistical report appears that purports to present the "latest truth" about illiteracy in the United States.

Six years ago, the Census Bureau cheerfully announced that 99.5 percent of all our citizens could read and write. Two years later, Barbara Bush, Vice President George Bush's wife, said that 60 million (33 percent of adults) could do neither very well. A year later, the White House said "our nation is at risk" because of the collapse in literacy skills. Then Terrel Bell, Secretary of Education at the time, told Congress that the literacy of more than 70 million adults must be viewed as "marginal" at best.

Six months ago, the Census Bureau made front pages with a study that identified "21 million" illiterates—give or take three million. A month ago, ABC News, in consensual despair, settled on "20 million" but hedged its bet by adding that it might be "40 million."

New Study

The other day, reporters had to dig into yet another study, from a Princeton group known as the National Assessment of Educational Progress. It reported that "only" 10 million adults were illiterate but that 36 million could not read at an eighth-grade level and that 70 million could not read as well as students in eleventh grade.

Where does this leave the humble citizen who is trying to figure it all out? The handling of the Princeton study demonstrates why the public is perplexed. The report was released at a press conference in which we were advised to "celebrate" the fact that we are doing well by "yesterday's standards" and in comparison to Third World nations. This is the part that made the headlines.

Disturbing Disclosures

Lost in a thicket of statistical verbosity and graphs that only the bold or hyperactive dared penetrate were truly disturbing disclosures. Forty percent of adults cannot make use of a road map; 80 percent can't calculate a tip in a restaurant or figure out which bus will get them home by using a schedule that is no more difficult than the ones most of us decipher every day.

17

SOVIET EDUCATION

Russia, at the time of the Revolution, was 75 percent illiterate, in remote areas 90-95 percent. Russia was the only European country which didn't have a law about compulsory elementary education. Only 10 percent of the children went to school, and those children were from wealthy families. According to the estimates of Tsarist officials, compulsory elementary education would not be possible until the year 2000! The Great Socialist Revolution of 1917 eliminated this old-fashioned and unequal system of education, and reconstructed it on a socialist basis:

1) education is free of charge at all levels with stipends, clothing, and textbooks supplied;

2) teaching is done in the native language—there are 100 different nationalities, and many of these did not even have their own written language; teaching is done in 54 languages, and books are published in 54 languages;

3) there are no private or religious schools—there is one common school and curriculum for every child;

4) there is no discrimination on any basis—sex, race, or nationality.

The Soviet Union has eliminated illiteracy.

Dr. Zoya Malkova, director of the Institute of General Pedagogy of the Academy of Sciences, speaking at the University of Minnesota on April 28, 1986

Despite these disclosures, the authors of the study did not hesitate to tell us that its findings were cause for celebration. Book-industry leaders, who have seen sales go flat in recent years and have seen B. Dalton, our preeminent bookseller, and Doubleday, one of our finest publishers, go up for sale because of a loss of readers, will find little to celebrate.

Lovers of the English language who believe the nation's cultural resilience is endangered by a population that will never read the words of Emerson, Walt Whitman, or Thoreau will not be breaking out champagne.

A spokesman for the Princeton study told the press that American society should be proud that it is the world's most literate. Such jingoistic foolishness pampers our ego but betrays our national self-interest.

By Bruce Beattie, *Daytona Beach News Journal* © 1986 Copley News Service. By permission of Copley News Service.

Book sales in the United States are 24th worldwide. Newspapers sales, calculated by the papers sold per thousand residents, provide the following comparison: United States, 269; West Germany, 408; Japan, 575.

Loss of readership means loss of competition. The number of cities with competing dailies has declined from 181 to 30 since 1947. Fifty-four daily papers have gone to their deaths since 1979.

The Message

What is the message? Not by "yesterday's standards" but today's, not by Third World standards but American criteria, readers competent to understand the written press and find enjoyment in simple verse are an endangered species.

As we honor the bicentennial of the Constitution, few will wish to celebrate the fact, embedded in the new report, that 70 million voters cannot read it. This reality remains as the dust of instant headlines gradually subsides. It will no doubt be clouded soon by the next "authoritative" study.

Despite the pressures of competition and deadlines, it would be desirable, next time around, for journalists to have enough time to present a story devoid of statistical narcotics that induce a false euphoria, which inevitably is followed by equally exaggerated anguish.

3 THE ILLITERACY PROBLEM

THE LIGHTS OF LITERACY ARE GOING OUT

Kevin J. Kelley

The following reading, by Kevin J. Kelley, discusses America's low literacy rates and examines the government's response to the problem. The article appeared in Guardian, *a radical journal of social and political opinion.*

Points to Consider:

1. How many Americans are classified as "functionally or marginally illiterate"?
2. According to the Census Bureau, what percentage of Americans can read or write?
3. How much does illiteracy cost the government?
4. What is the correlation between reading competence and political participation?
5. What actions point to U.S. government indifference in responding to the illiteracy problem?

Kevin J. Kelley, "All Over the U.S., the Lights of Literacy are Going Out," *Guardian*, March 27, 1985, p. 7.

***Despite such glaring indications of a "national securi-
ty" problem, federal authorities have done very little
to promote adult literacy.***

Every day, millions of adults in the U.S. find themselves unable to
perform the following tasks: reading the directions on a medicine label;
computing their change at the grocery store; filling out a job application; understanding food stamp eligibility rules; reviewing a child's
homework assignment; making sense of a hospital's hysterectomy con-
sent form; deciphering the page-one headline in a tabloid.

They are among the estimated 33 percent of all Americans 18 years
of age or older who are classified as "functionally or marginally illiterate."
Of this 60 million total, nearly half cannot read or calculate at even a
rudimentary level. The remainder, states progressive educator Jonathan
Kozol in his book *Illiterate America* (Doubleday, 1985), "read only at
a level which is less than equal to the full survival needs of our society."

Some researchers believe there are actually many more than 60
million de facto illiterates in the U.S. In fact, no one knows precisely
how many adult citizens lack essential English reading comprehension
skills, but as best as can be determined, some 16 percent of whites,
44 percent of blacks, and 56 percent of Latinos fall into this category,
with females representing about 60 percent of the total. And the situation appears to be steadily worsening, especially among minorities. For
example, almost half of all black 17-year-olds are now unable to meet
those basic "survival needs."

Census Bureau Findings

This picture of a nation one-third illiterate bears no resemblance to
the latest Census Bureau finding that 99.5 percent of all adult Americans
can read and write. That official figure, submitted to world bodies for
purposes of national comparisons, is based on the patently dubious
assumption that anyone completing fifth grade should be considered
literate.

From 1940 to 1970, Kozol points out, the Census Bureau did not even
bother to measure literacy rates. It began doing so again, in its current
unhelpful manner, as a result of pressure from the armed forces which
had discovered that a lot more than .5 percent of its recruits could not
read or write in any meaningful sense.

National Security Problem

Despite such glaring indications of a "national security" problem,
federal authorities have done very little to promote adult literacy. In 1973,
the Nixon administration did indirectly acknowledge that a crisis existed

A NATIONAL SHAME

Illiteracy is unquestionably a national shame and unless we do something about it, the problem is likely to get worse instead of better with society's increasing emphasis on information-oriented, high technology.

Excerpted from Congressional testimony of Representative Augustus F. Hawkins, chairman of the Committee on Education and Labor, September 30, 1986

when it launched a "Right to Read" campaign. It was virtually abandoned six years later, however, with its director terming the effort a failure.

The Reagan White House announced its own "Adult Literacy Initiative" in September 1983, but it sought only $360,000 in new funding for the President's pledge to wipe out illiteracy. The government now spends about $100 million a year on adult reading and writing programs, compared to the $5 billion that will be required in order to bring about a substantial improvement in national literacy standards, according to the head of the National Advisory Council on Adult Education. As has been the case with so many social problems, the Reagan administration poses individual and corporate voluntarism as the solution to illiteracy.

A report released in December by Librarian of Congress Daniel Boorstin, who is supposed to be one of the nation's pre-eminent monitors of intellectual standards, offered "encouraging examples of what we all can do" to help abolish illiteracy in the U.S. by 1989. Among the suggestions were installation of a "family library" in the White House and putting blurbs on cereal boxes to publicize bookish TV shows. Boorstin, wrote Ken Ringle, of the *Washington Post,* was "questioned by reporters who appeared uniformly confused by the report."

Government Indifference

Such governmental responses cause some activists in the field to wonder whether low literacy rates are not in fact being deliberately fostered and ignored.

The effects of such widespread incapacity to cope with contemporary life seem, in some ways, to be inimical to ruling-class interests. Kozol estimates that illiteracy costs the government $20 billion a year in the form of welfare, unemployment compensation, and prison maintenance outlays directly attributable to individuals' lack of reading skills. The *Wall Street Journal* meanwhile reports that corporations are now conduct-

ing their own literacy courses in an attempt to stem the productivity losses resulting from employees' poor comprehension levels.

At the same time, the systemic causes of illiteracy and its disproportionate incidence among minorities suggest more than just a "policy problem." Urging reduced federal spending on schools, a writer for the Heritage Foundation warned in 1983, for example, that "overeducation" might lead to "greater discontent and still lower productivity."

Why is the government so indifferent to the fact that 45 percent of the country's adults do not read a daily newspaper and that the U.S. ranks 24th internationally in books published per capita? Those statistics point to the presumed high correlation between reading competence and political participation. It also seems likely that people who cannot comprehend critical writings are most susceptible to the sort of visual manipulation that now characterizes most electoral campaigns.

"Democracy is a mendacious term when used by those who are prepared to countenance the forced exclusion" from informed political activity of a third of the adult citizenry, writes Kozol.

The U.S. government's performance in combating illiteracy can be tellingly contrasted to successful campaigns undertaken in the Third World, especially in non-capitalist countries such as Cuba and Nicaragua. Universal literacy and numeracy is widely regarded there as a prerequisite for emancipation, empowerment, and economic advance.

It should also be noted that UNESCO (United Nation's Educational Scientific and Cultural Organization) has been a principal sponsor of some of the most fruitful literacy projects in the developing world. This is the UN agency from which Washington withdrew last year, complaining of its "politicization."

Thousands Turned Away

At home, too, the U.S. government thwarts the desire of millions to learn to read and write. All the adult literacy programs in this country reach, at most, 4 percent of the population in need. In Illinois alone,

140,000 people have sought to enroll in literacy courses but have been turned away due to a lack of funding.

Simply enrolling in a class is, meanwhile, no automatic guarantee of success. With four hours of constructive training per week for one year, an adult's reading level can usually be raised by two grades, according to Michael Fox, director of Push Literacy Action Now, a highly praised volunteer project in Washington, D.C. Some courses do not, however, provide useful instruction, leading to student frustration and high drop-out rates. One of the main causes of such failure, states Fox, "is that many educators feel there is something wrong with their students rather than with their programs."

Lifelong Neglect

Meanwhile, the darkness spreads. Public schools do little to counter illiteracy's tendency to reproduce itself over generations. The child of parents who cannot read or write will seldom attain real competence without concerted and creative intervention in the classroom. But few schools have the funding or the administrative commitment needed to insure intensive instruction, instead shunting pupils from grade to grade until they either abandon the system or are handed a meaningless "certificate of attendance."

The results of such lifelong neglect, insofar as they are known, offer some hint of the desperation associated with illiteracy:

- 85 percent of the children brought before family court are classified as "severely disabled readers";

- Up to 70 percent of the long-term unemployed do not possess the basic intellectual tools required for job retraining;

- Half of the (mostly female) heads of households below the official poverty line cannot read an eighth grade book;

- A third of the mothers receiving Aid to Families with Dependent Children are functionally illiterate.

"One of the most precious rights assured to U.S. citizens is freedom of the press," writes Kozol, but widespread illiteracy makes it "a questionable guarantee," he observes. "People are free to choose what they believe, but freedom to choose depends on prior knowledge of the choices."

4 THE ILLITERACY PROBLEM

ILLITERACY ISN'T REALLY A PROBLEM

Patrick Cox and Jeff Riggenbach

The following comments by Patrick Cox and Jeff Riggenbach were reprinted from USA Today.

Patrick Cox is the publisher of *SIGnet Magazine*, a high-tech entertainment bi-monthly. Jeff Riggenbach is an editorial writer and columnist for the *Orange County Register.*

Points to Consider:

1. Explain why literacy standards are ethnocentric.
2. What are the flaws in the literacy formula?
3. Who is crying out over the problem of adult illiteracy and why?
4. Should government spend more money to combat illiteracy? Why or why not?

by Patrick Cox

Those losing sleep over reports that too many people in the USA aren't able to read might as well worry that people in the USA aren't able to reproduce. Those who really want to usually find a way to do it. Those who don't want to just can't be forced to buy newspapers.

Nobody takes the dairy industry seriously when it complains that we aren't drinking enough milk. Similarly, there's no reason to worry when the reading industry exaggerates its fears of a declining customer base. I would be suspicious about the print media complaining about illiteracy even if I believed the illiteracy statistics used. And I do not.

Ethnocentric Standards

One popular definition of illiteracy is not being able to read sixth-grade level materials. Another sets the level at the twelfth grade. The first and most fundamental flaw in these standards is that literacy is often judged only in English. Millions of immigrants are considered illiterate by these ethnocentric standards, even though they are often bilingual.

Consider the immigrant experience: individuals and families give up their cultures, languages, customs, and friends to seek the opportunity presented in the USA. Statistics clearly show that second-generation immigrants are better educated and make more money than the U.S. national average. Does it really make sense to worry about the reading habits of a group that will almost certainly outperform more sedentary natives within a few years?

The Literacy Formula

The refusal of some to accept the nature of supposedly illiterate immigrants' accomplishments, simply because they do not read and write English, is not only racist, it ignores the common roots of all of us. Further, immigrants' success points out the importance that initiative plays in the literacy formula. Parents who can't read their children's English birth certificates often send those same children to the best universities in the USA.

If immigrants can overcome the burdens they face to learn to read, we must face the fact that many others who do not pass literacy tests simply have no interest in doing so. That is the second flaw in the illiteracy formula. Lots of people don't *want* to read, and nothing can be done to change their values.

Self-serving Groups

I'm not surprised when bureaucrats and educators who have to justify their jobs raise the specter of rampant illiteracy. But when the print media joins in, it embarrasses me. It reveals a blindness about the nature of societal evolution that ought to be a part of journalism's consciousness.

26

Furthermore, the bottom line is predictable: Newspaper chains are not going to start offering classes to those who wish to improve their reading skills. They are going to ask for more taxes to be spent on what is essentially a subsidy to their industry. And who's going to pay for it? Read my lips.

by Jeff Riggenbach

The truth about adult illiteracy in the USA is that no one knows exactly how widespread it is.

But we do know that the available figures are absurdly exaggerated, that the seriousness of the problem is likewise exaggerated, and that government is the very last place we should look for solutions to those problems with illiteracy that actually do exist.

How Many Illiterates?

Everyone who decries the problem of adult illiteracy stresses the shame adult illiterates feel and their efforts to conceal the problem not only from strangers but even from their own families.

But if adult illiterates will not admit to their illiteracy, how can anyone possibly know how many of them there are?

Functional Illiterates

The statistics we've all seen, putting the illiterate adult population at anywhere from 17 million to 60 million, are based on the inability of *literate* people to do as well on written tests as the testers think they ought to do. This is called "functional illiteracy." In fact, it isn't illiteracy at all, and calling it that is presumptuous.

The only person truly qualified to decide how well any given individual needs to be able to read and write in order to function satisfactorily

27

ILLITERACY IN LATIN AMERICA

Sixteen Latin American countries, including Puerto Rico, show an average illiteracy rate of 21.6 percent.

The rate covers a total of 43,032,591 adults, of whom 21,015,244 (48.8 percent) are women.

The countries with the highest illiteracy rate are in Central America. Guatemala heads the list with 56.6 percent (3,800,000 adults), trailed by Honduras with 40.5 percent (706,659) and El Salvador with 37.9 percent (1,700,000).

The South American countries with the highest illiteracy rate are Bolivia, with 36.8 percent (993,437) and Columbia, with 34.0 (7,000,000).

Literacy programs are being put into effect in several of the countries included in the study, in some cases with the country's own resources and in others with the assistance of such international organizations as UNESCO.

The following table gives a general view on illiteracy in the 16 countries:

Countries	Rate of illiteracy	Number of illiterates	Number of illiterate women
Bolivia	36.8 (1)	993,437 (2)	716,858 (3)
Brazil	21.9	17,204,041	9,293,712
Chile	6.0	650,000	------ (4)
Colombia	34.0	7,000,000 (5)	3,920,000
Costa Rica	6.0	115,000	55,000
Ecuador	15.6 (6)	738,000	442,800
El Salvador	37.9	1,700,000	884,000
Guatemala	56.6	3,800,000	------ (7)
Honduras	40.5	706,659	370,487
Mexico	17.0	6,451,740	3,906,569
Nicaragua	12.0	60,000	33,000
Panama	13.2	174,125	89,610
Peru	18.0	1,799,000	467,740
Puerto Rico	11.5	277,185	------ (8)
Uruguay	7.1	161,494	88,261
Venezuela	12.0	1,201,910	747,207
16 countries	21.6	43,032,591	21,015,244 (9)

1) Other sources estimate 55 percent.
2) 1976 figure.
3) 1983 figure.
4) No data available.
5) In Colombia seven million people cannot read or write; 2.5 million are absolutely illiterate; 0.5 million boys and girls (10-to-14 age bracket) have never gone to school; and four million are functionally illiterate.
6) For persons of 15 years or more the rate is 15.6.
7) No data available, yet it is estimated that the number of illiterate women exceeds that of men.
8) No data available.
9) Women represent 46.8 percent of all illiterates.

Gramma Weekly Review, *February 24, 1986*

in our society is that individual—the one doing the reading, writing, and functioning.

Between one-third and one-half of all the people the U.S. Department of Education calls "illiterate" are foreign-born and do not speak English at home. Most of them are quite literate in some other language and most of them live in areas where literacy in English is not required in order to function satisfactorily.

What's the Fuss?

Why are so many people wringing their hands over a problem that can't be meaningfully quantified and is probably almost non-existent? Because they know what side their bread is buttered on. The loudest voices crying out over the problem of adult illiteracy belong to people in the publishing industry who fear erosion of their customer base and to people in the education business who know that stirring up public outrage over illiteracy may put them in line for lucrative grants from private foundations and from government.

How private foundations spend their money is nobody's business but theirs and their doners'.

But how government spends its money is everyone's business, since government gets its money by robbing all of us.

Those who call for government to spend a hundred times what it is already spending to combat adult illiteracy seem to forget one of the most important lessons of federal education policy over the past two decades.

During that time, government expenditures per pupil increased by several hundred percent, and the result was that test scores and every other measure of educational accomplishment steadily declined.

However many adult illiterates there may really be out there, if we authorize government to throw money at them, their numbers will only increase.

29

UNDERSTANDING ILLITERACY

This activity may be used an an individualized study guide for students in libraries and resource centers or as a discussion catalyst in small group and classroom discussions.

The following is an exact typed copy of a handwritten letter that Jonathan Kozol, author of *Illiterate America,* received from a scarcely literate woman. Read the letter carefully and answer the questions on the next page.

A fure nights ago I happen to chuch the last 10.min of your show. And I think you were talking about people like me. You keep talking about reading AND writing. Well I have a spelling problem. I say spelling because when you try to fine help in spelling you dont fine it in a writing class.

Since grade school my teacher would say you need to leard to spell. AND yet they never been able to teach me. So they'll say maybe youwl leard next year. I took english and writing classes and they dont teach you anlything.

So as the years gone by the more one has to hide once problem as you mention. As one try to fine ways to improve.

When I finsh hight school I thought I wasnt good enife fo college. But I didn't want to be a nobody—They say education is the way to anlything. So I went to college AND found there were quite alot of other people like me. But geting through college wasent easle. Some time you have to repeat a class. I repeated classes 3 times be for giving upon making it.

You hear people say no you cant take this because you dont make the grades. You never make it. But I keep trying because I want to be a better person. Im not ready to settle down to a factory job. I have hight intrest. I know I can do the job—but the spelling trows a lot of problem.

Im 33 now and finly have made a go. But the walls are up agent. and this time I dont think I can go around them. What Im I to do. I still have some engeny left. But runing out. Im afrade to run out—I dont know if I can settle for noting.

Whats the problem—I finly graduated as a surgical Tech. I can do the job well I know what Im doing. But If I have to put anlything down on papper Im lost. I repeated my medical Term 3 times because of spelling. And work very hard to make it through my testes. Now Im a graduate it is best that one take ther certifacation test. Im afrade to take it and would preferd not too. The chances of geting this job would be to take this test. But not for me. It cost $200 to take it on top of other things. One still can get a job with out it but very slim now days. Even thought times are hard they still ask to take it.

I feel its just another way to block us out. We belive in ourself we try to improve there mist teaching—we suffer now putg money after money in to try to improve ourself. But thats all we do is spend what little we have in hope for a dream.

People like us belong in a factory or cleang or table jobs. But Im not happy with these job. Sure there perfet one dont have to prove introlet. But its not for me—I finly found some thing after two other major. But the walls are up. . .

The school has a spelling class that I would like to take. But the timeng hasn't been right at the moment. Im not sure this class will teach me what I need . . .

The teaching system is importion—I came to you as a child—you fail me I come as an adult—you still fail me I bring my child to you—For I can not teach than I ask please do not do to them what you have done to me—we are crying teach me I have some thing to offer but first I need to leard.

Points to Consider:

1. What is the writer saying in this letter?

2. The writer says she has a spelling problem. What other problems do you see?

3. How do you think the writer was able to graduate from high school without being able to spell? How was she able to graduate as a surgical technician? What does this say about the writer and her attitude? What does this say about society?

4. Describe the fears and concerns the writer has for herself and for her child.

CHAPTER 2

DEALING WITH ILLITERACY

5 DEALING WITH ILLITERACY

EXPAND FEDERAL SUPPORT

Donald A. McCune

Dr. Donald A. McCune is the director of Adult, Alternative, and Continuation Education Services Division for the California State Department of Education. He is also active in both the American Association of Adult and Continuing Education (AAACE) and the National Council of State Directors of Adult Education.

Points to Consider:

1. How does the author describe the nature of the illiteracy problem?
2. What inadequacies must be overcome in providing literacy services?
3. Why does the author recommend funding Section 309 of the Adult Education Act?
4. What additional observations does the author make concerning illiteracy?

Excerpted from testimony of Donald A. McCune before the House Subcommittee on Elementary, Secondary, and Vocational Education of the House Committee on Education and Labor, October 3, 1985.

Being literate is an empowerment of an individual that helps to remove barriers to achievement and contributes to our future as a free people. Both public and private sectors must accept responsibility for providing resources and leadership at the national level.

The following is a brief attempt to identify some of the critical factors which must be considered in any strategic planning for reducing levels of illiteracy. I will conclude with recommendations for initiating actions leading to supporting existing literacy services and developing new approaches of response.

The Nature of the Problem

Illiteracy has gained increasing attention in the last few years because of compelling evidence that the number of adult illiterates is large and growing steadily and also because of a recognition that people lacking literacy skills represent almost every level and segment of society. Although the increased level of demand for literacy services is very important and must be addressed, the developing awareness of the diversity of the illiterate population is a relatively new factor calling for the attention of those developing and implementing policies that will facilitate responsive literacy services. With those in need coming from such diverse backgrounds, it is imperative that we develop and maintain parallel diversity in the delivery of literacy services.

Another observation of the nature of the problem of illiteracy is that it is not an issue which is likely to respond to short-term solutions. The numbers of those now needing literacy services, the rate at which illiteracy seems to be growing, and the complexity of motivating and maintaining client-interest and involvement in the learning process mitigate against any immediate resolution of illiteracy in the United States. Illiteracy is part of a much larger socioeconomic problem. Sticht (1983), for example, comments that illiteracy is transmitted from generation to generation through the process of illiterate parents and their children.

A final factor which must be noted here is the recognition that illiteracy is an issue which must be considered on a national level as well as at state and local levels. The impact of illiteracy upon this nation's economic, political, and social well-being is unquestionable. Being literate is an empowerment of an individual that helps to remove barriers to achievement and contributes to our future as a free people. Both public and private sectors must accept responsibility for providing resources and leadership at the national level.

34

Current Efforts to Provide Literacy Services

The infrastructure supporting the delivery of literacy services is characterized by a wide range and variety of providers and conditions of accessibility. Harman (1985), Kozol (1985), and McCune and Alamprese (1985) have considered the provision of literacy services and identified those that appear to constitute a national effort in this regard. There is general agreement among their reports and studies that this effort includes the services and programs of: (1) the federal government through the Adult Education Act, programs for military personnel, and activities related to job training and employment preparation; (2) public school and community colleges; (3) voluntary organizations such as Laubach Literacy Action and Literacy Volunteers of America; (4) libraries; (5) business, industry, and organized labor; (6) community-based organizations; and (7) correctional institutions and systems.

The success of these efforts can only be measured against the level of limited resources available, their separateness and the lack of articulation among the programs, the increasing demands for services, and the limited availability of those with expertise and experience in organizing and providing literacy services. I believe that under these conditions our current efforts are doing very well.

An overall assessment of the existing efforts as compared to the extent of the problem clearly reveals the inadequacies that must be overcome. Quite simply, more people need to be served; the scope of service needs to be expanded to serve a broader range of clients; there is a need to articulate existing services to maximize effectiveness, training, and staff development, which are needed to improve the quality and quantity of services; and we must have an appropriate statement of national policy on this issue to guide the establishment of priorities and the allocation of resources which will assure a future commitment to the development of a literate nation.

By Bill Sanders, *Milwaukee Journal* © 1986 News America Syndicate by permission of North America Syndicate, Inc.

Recommendations

The preceding discussion of the nature of the problem and the current status of literacy efforts form the basis for proposing the following for your consideration.

The most immediate need is to expand the capacity of those now providing literacy services. This will require a significant increase in funding. The Adult Education Act in its present form is an appropriate mechanism for quickly responding to this need for rapid growth. It has provisions for the support of community-based, voluntary, and institutional programs as well as the efforts of public schools and community colleges. The diversity of program providers must be encouraged to assure the availability of a mutiplicity of programs that will attract and retain a variety of client groups.

Section 309 of the Adult Education Act should be funded to enable the U.S. Department of Education to support specific activities in program development, demonstration, dissemination, research, and evaluation leading to more effective and comprehensive literacy services.

Support is needed to establish a national center or institute for adult learning. Such a facility would be able to provide a wide-range of functions and services necessary to focus on the needs of literacy programs and providers. Fostering communication among the provider systems, gathering and disseminating knowledge about adult literacy, articulating needs for research and development, and amassing information and data vital to the formulation of national and state policies would be some of the most important contributions.

Encouragement is needed to expand the technical assistance services of the U.S. Department of Education and the departments of education in the states. Guidelines for the types of services and the extension of their availability to non-traditional delivery systems should be provided and emphasized.

Some Additional Observations

Rather than summarizing this discussion on illiteracy, I would like to conclude with some observations that stand apart and need to be taken by themselves as they might apply to this issue.

1. The importance of the illiteracy cycle calls for renewed efforts to emphasize programs for illiterate parents. Attention to specialized recruitment techniques and the development of unique curriculum and instructional approaches should assist in this focused effort.

2. Mechanisms are needed to provide for the transference of information on effective literacy programs and materials from one delivery system to another.

3. Quality education in our elementary and secondary schools continues to be the single most important intervention in reducing levels of illiteracy in our adult populations.

4. The role of technology in promoting literacy remains unclear. We are beginning to gather experience with this potentially effective tool in the acquisition of literacy. There is much to learn about the effects of our present technology on the individual as well as on the development of literacy skills.

5. We still need to consider the fact that the basic literacy skills of reading, composition, and computation need to be placed in a context of usefulness in an adult's daily life. It is the ability to apply these skills that ultimately determines success.

References

Sticht, T.G. (1983). *Literacy and Human Resources Development at Work: Investing in the Education of Adults to Improve the Educability of Children.* Alexandria, Virginia: Human Resources Research Organization.

Kozol, Jonathan (1985). *Illiterate America.* New York: Anchor Press/Doubleday.

McCune, D.A. and Alamprese, J.A. (1985). *Turning Illiteracy Around: An Agenda for National Action.* Working Paper No. 1. New York: Business Council for Effective Literacy.

Harman, David (1985). *Turning Illiteracy Around: An Agenda for National Action.* Working Paper No. 2. New York: Business Council for Effective Literacy.

6 DEALING WITH ILLITERACY

INCREASED FEDERAL AID WILL NOT WORK

Barry Goldwater

Barry Goldwater is a retired United States senator from Arizona and a former chairman of the Committee on Armed Services. Mr. Goldwater was also a co-sponsor of an amendment to identify the causes of illiteracy in the early years of education (kindergarten through third grade).

Points to Consider:

1. Why is Senator Goldwater baffled by schools that seek federal funds for remedial programs?
2. What reason does Senator Goldwater offer as an explanation for the Gallego School's success in reading, grammar, and math?
3. Why did the Reading Reform Foundation receive 25,000 letters in response to the *Reader's Digest* editorial?
4. According to the Department of Education's report *What Works: Research about Teaching and Learning,* how does the phonics method work?

Excerpted from testimony of Barry Goldwater before the House Subcommittee on Elementary, Secondary, and Vocational Education of the House Committee on Education and Labor, March 20, 1986.

Our children deserve the best we have to offer. What better gift to give our young people than the ability to decode the written word.

It is my firm belief that a discussion on illiteracy is without the heart of the argument if the prevention of illiteracy is not a major focus of the discussion. Unfortunately, there are over 23 million Americans who are considered illiterate. I do not deny the tremendous need for remedial reading programs to help these people. My concern is to prevent this incredible statistic from increasing by even one more American.

Federal Funding Not Necessary

We cannot continue to talk about illiteracy without asking the question: "How is beginning reading being taught in our schools?" Our young Americans start school eager and ready to learn and for many of these children the healthy spirit of adventure into the world of school and learning quickly changes. Many are labeled learning disabled and placed in classes apart from their homeroom. Parents need to question whether a child has a true learning problem or whether the child has been taught by an ineffective and inefficient reading program. It is one of the most baffling situations I know of that schools readily seek federal funds for remedial programs. I believe the need for such programs indicates a lack of success in the instructional program of the school. I grant you that some students will need special assistance through a remedial program, but I hope the percentage of students in these programs would be relatively low.

The Gallego School

The Gallego School in the Sunnyside School District of South Tucson in Arizona provides a concrete example. The principal of Gallego, Mrs. Musgrave, chose to receive no federal funds for the school. It is a kindergarten through sixth grade basics school with an intensive phonics program for its mostly Hispanic, lower socioeconomic student body. Many of the households do not have a working parent, but the school, with its dress and discipline codes, is fully supported by the parents. Many of these parents themselves do not speak fluent English; however, they want no special treatment for themselves or their children.

Gallego uses the Iowa Test of Basic Skills and the school ranks number one out of 16 schools in the Sunnyside District with reading, grammar, and math above grade levels in all six grades. It should be noted that there are 522 students and 22 teachers. There are no specialists on the Gallego faculty. The morning schedule is core time: three hours of uninterrupted classroom instruction with a concentration on phonics skills in the lower grades.

The Gallego school chose to use the Spalding Phonics Program. The teachers at Gallego were taught by Mrs. Spalding herself. Also, the Spalding Phonics Program is the program of choice of the Reading Reform Foundation of Scottsdale, Arizona. I am proud to report the foundation has chapters across the country and the Scottsdale facility is the national headquarters. Each chapter has an opportunity to utilize a phonics program of their choice, so not every program uses the Spalding method. The Spalding method has been repeatedly proven to be both cost-effective and time efficient. The cost can be considered nominal as there are few materials needed and it is easily taught to lay people as well as to teachers who do not feel they can effectively teach beginning reading. One of the major functions of the foundation, founded by parents and educators in 196l, is to provide a systematic, multi-sensory phonics program for beginning reading instruction.

Reader's Digest Editorial

In November 1985, *Reader's Digest* published an editorial on illiteracy entitled "Why Children Aren't Reading." At the close of the editorial, the postscript stated: "For more information about teaching reading by the phonics method," and gave the address of the Reading Reform Foundation in Scottsdale, Arizona. Mrs. Bettina Rubicam, president of the foundation, a dear friend, and tireless worker in the fight for literacy, told me that the foundation received over 25,000 letters as a result of the *Reader's Digest* editorial. These letters had not only been sent by concerned individuals from across the country, but also from around the world. This kind of response tells me there are many individuals who are deeply concerned with the problems of illiteracy and they want to learn what beginning reading programs work. They are not looking for gimmicks and extensive materials—just give them what works.

Doug MacGregor's cartoons appear regularly in the Norwich, Conn., Bulletin

Copyright 1986, *USA Today.* Reprinted with permission.

Phonics: Answer to Reading Dilemma?

The *Reader's Digest* editorial stated that a beginning reading program needs to have an intensive phonics component. The *Reader's Digest* phonics recommendation supported and gave credit to *Becoming a Nation of Readers: The Report of the Commission on Reading,* which was sponsored by the Department of Education. This report stated in its own recommendations that: "Teachers of beginning reading should present well-designed phonics instruction." It went on to state: "Though most children today are taught phonics, often this instruction is poorly conceived." According to Richard C. Anderson, chairman of this commission, "The report contains the most thoughtful, scholarly, and comprehensive statement that has ever been made about the nature of reading and the practices in the home and the school that promote literacy."

In addition to this strong recommendation for intensive phonics instruction in beginning reading programs, the Department of Education released its latest report entitled: *What Works: Research About Teaching and Learning.* I would like to quote the section on phonics in its entirety as it gives not only research findings, but also provides important background information on how we arrived at our present reading dilemma:

> Children get a better start in reading if they are taught phonics. Learning phonics helps them to understand the relationship between letters and sounds and to 'break the code' that links the words they hear with the words they see in print.
>
> Until the 1930s and 1940s, most American children learned to read by the phonics method, which stresses the relationships between spoken sounds and printed letters. Children learned the letters of the alphabet and the sounds those letters represent. For several decades thereafter, however, the 'Look-Say' approach to reading was dominant: Children were taught to identify whole words in the belief that they would make more rapid progress if they identified whole words at a glance, as adults seem to. Recent research indicates that, on the average, children who are taught phonics get off to a better start in learning to read than children who are not taught phonics.
>
> Identifying words quickly and accurately is one of the cornerstones of skilled reading. Phonics improves the ability of children both to identify words and to sound out new ones. Sounding out the letters in a word is like the first tentative steps of a toddler: It helps children gain a secure verbal footing and expand their vocabularies beyond the limits of basic readers.
>
> Because phonics is a reading tool, it is best taught in the context of reading instruction, not as a separate subject to be mastered. Good phonics strategies include teaching children the sounds of letters in isolation and in words (s/i/t), and how to blend the sounds together (s-s-i-i-t).
>
> Phonics should be taught early but not over-used. If phonics instruction extends for too many years, it can defeat the spirit and excitement of learning to read. Phonics helps children pronounce words approximately, a skill they can learn by the end of second grade. In the meantime, children can learn to put their new phonics skills to work by reading good stories and poems.

Senator Goldwater's Challenge

Although I do not always find myself in favor of the Department of Education's reports, I feel compelled to commend the efforts of Secretary Bennett and Assistant Secretary Finn for these reports. I believe the reports achieved their goals of gathering pertinent and tested knowledge on education and of widely disseminating the information in laymen's terms. I now challenge the Department of Education, as I have challenged the Department of Defense, to find waste and abuse and to stop funding programs that do not work. The American public deserves a fair return on its tax dollars. Concrete results in reading scores and a reduction in the number of children being placed in remedial reading programs would be a step in the right direction.

Our schools should not be turning out losers, but rather making every child a winner. Many of us are constantly stating how valuable our children are, but they are also extremely vulnerable. At a time when they are both young and vulnerable, it seems unfair to expect so much from them. They are repeatedly tested, but our society seems to demand these tests.

Well, if we are going to test our young at least give them a chance to succeed by using proven programs that are both effective and efficient in the transfer of knowledge. It is my hope the above reports on phonics and education and the upcoming hearing on the prevention of illiteracy will be the necessary forces to require all local educational agencies to provide an intensive phonics component in beginning reading instruction. Our children deserve the best we have to offer. What better gift to give our young people than the ability to decode the written word.

44

A NATIONAL CAMPAIGN
TO END ILLITERACY

Jonathan Kozol

Jonathan Kozol graduated from Harvard in 1958 and attended Oxford on a Rhodes Scholarship. In the fall of 1964, he began teaching in the Boston Public Schools at the elementary level. Out of his experience came Death At An Early Age, *which won the National Book Award in Science, Philosophy & Religion. Supported by the Rockefeller and Guggenheim foundations, he wrote* Illiterate America, *published by Doubleday.*

Points to Consider:

1. The author reports that last May the Pentagon was forced to "write down" manuals. What does the term "write down" mean? How much will it cost to "write down" manuals for the B-1 bomber program?
2. What group represents the majority of illiterate Americans?
3. How do community programs help illiterates overcome their anxiety and terror of humiliation?
4. What specific recommendations does the author provide?

Excerpted from testimony of Jonathan Kozol before the House Subcommittee on Elementary, Secondary, and Vocational Education of the House Committee on Education and Labor, October 3, 1985.

*Federal support for local literacy action may well repre-
sent the one good cause on which conservatives and
liberals, rich and poor, the business-minded and the
socially committed may wholeheartedly agree.*

I will speak only briefly of the numbers that confront us and the
measurable costs to our society. My major concern is with the costs
that are not measurable. I have in mind the limitless price that is ex-
acted from the children of illiterate adults and the deepening burden
that this places on the public schools. I will propose that only programs
centered in the neighborhoods in which such people live, and organized
in ways that can invite and then reward their rapid and unhesitant participation, have much chance of making an important dent upon the
challenge that we face.

Illiterate America: What is the Problem?

It would be understandable if members of Congress were bewildered
by the many conflicting numbers that are cited. It may simplify this issue
greatly if it can be understood that almost all of these disputes are
arguments of definition rather than of numbers. Over 25 million adults
read below the fifth grade level: a competence essential for survival
and employment of the most conventional kind. At least another 35
million read beneath the ninth grade level. Newspapers are written at
between the tenth and twelfth grade levels. It requires ninth grade competence to understand the antidote instructions on a can of kitchen
cleanser, tenth grade competence to understand instructions on a
federal income tax return, twelfth grade competence to read a life insurance form. Blue-collar manuals used in factories require better than
a tenth grade reading level. Manuals for retraining of employees in the
high-tech industries call for much higher levels.

I have argued that all of these 60 million people therefore ought to
be regarded as "illiterate in terms of U.S. industry and print communication in the 1980s."

The largest cost in dollars is, of course, the heightened welfare burden
and the loss in productivity. While this cost defies precise enumera-
tion, it has been estimated in the tens of billions yearly. More specific
items have been documented: It was reported last May that the Pentagon is forced to "write down" manuals of instruction to be understood
by only semi-literate personnel. The cost of dumbing down the manuals
for the B-1 bomber program, for example, will exceed $1 billion.

Note one other large and rather saddening expense: 85 percent of
juveniles who come before the courts and 60 percent of prison inmates
read below the fifth grade level. Whatever this cost—and, even leaving
out the human price, we know it runs to many billions—we may note

46

that criminals do not respect state borders. We are all held hostage to each other in this nation. A national tragedy would appear to call for national response.

Disadvantaged Children

The toll taken on the children of nonreaders is my primary concern. There are several ways in which the children of illiterate adults are placed at disadvantage.

Illiterate parents, first of all, cannot provide their children with the model of adults who feel at ease with books; far from being at their ease, they are likely to regard books with anxiety.

Second, such parents cannot read to children during the crucial early years before they enter school.

Third, they frequently cannot afford to purchase books. The likelihood of personal embarrassment inhibits them, meanwhile, from making use of libraries and therefore holds their children at a distance from the library as well.

Fourth, they find it difficult to overcome uneasiness in contact with the public schools (scenes of remembered failure in their earlier years) and, for this reason, they forfeit their potential role in parent-teacher organizations or in private meetings with their child's teacher. Many cannot even read the notes sent home by teachers asking them to come in to discuss their children's needs.

Fifth, they have no opportunity to supervise their child's studies, to assist with homework, or to scrutinize curriculum or texts; nor, of course, can they assist their children in the preparation for examinations or in choice of courses needed for fulfillment of requirements for graduation.

Sixth, they lack the leverage of informed analysis by which to recognize the problems of a school or to assess the quality of teachers.

Finally, even when they do intuitively sense the warning signs of a deficient education, they can rarely turn their intuitions into positive and helpful criticisms phrased in literate and cogent terms that school officials will be likely to respect or even understand.

While all these factors undermine a child's opportunities for educational success, it is the parent's inability to take a role during the pre-school years which seems to be most keenly recognized and frequently discussed by the illiterate adults that I have known.

I have spoken in the past five years with hundreds of nonreaders in at least two dozen cities. Again and again, I ask the simple question: "Why do you want to read?" The three most common reasons that I hear reveal parental longings of a soaring eloquence, tied closely to a recognition of the cultural starvation which their children undergo.

"I want to read the Bible." That is repeatedly the first reply.

Almost as commonly, I hear this explanation: "I'd just like to understand good books."

Finally, and related closely to these reasons, I hear this: "I would like to help my children. I don't want to see them doomed to lead the life that I have had to live."

One mother worded it like this. "I can't read to them. Of course that's leaving them out of something they should have. My youngest, Donny, wanted me to read a book to him. I told Donny: 'I can't read.' I tried it one day, reading from the pictures. Donny looked at me. He said, 'Mommy, that's not right.' He's only five. He *knew* I couldn't read . . ." She sighed and then she said: "Oh, it matters! You *believe* it matters."

Another mother spoke these words: "I look at my 17-year-old son and my 12-year-old daughter and I want to help them with their homework, but I can't. My son was supposed to repeat the ninth grade for the third time this year . . . He finally said he wanted to drop out . . . I see my handicap being passed on to my son . . . I tell you, it scares me."

Prayers like these must not remain unanswered. Certain people tell us in censorious terms that our literacy problems would be helped if parents would fulfill their obligation to sit down and read books to their children. They do not explain how parents who cannot read for themselves can possibly assist their children.

I do not intend to bury you in numbers, but one body of statistics may be worth brief mention here. Illiteracy cuts across all ethnic lines. It is identified with poverty, not race. The vast majority of illiterate Americans are white and native-born. In the State of Utah, where the population is almost entirely white and native-born, 200,000 adults cannot read and write. For those who are nonwhite, however, and for this reason far more likely to be very poor, the percentages are disproportionately alarming. Sixteen percent of white adults, 44 percent of blacks, and 56 percent of all Hispanic adults are either total, functional, or marginal illiterates. Forty-seven percent of all black 17-year-olds are functionally illiterate. That figure is expected to rise to 50 percent by 1990. Women are more likely to be illiterate than men. Young nonwhite women for this reason represent the highest single concentration of illiterate adults.

With over half of nonwhite children growing up in single-parent, female-headed homes, it is realistic to expect that those who are their children stand in greatest jeopardy of entering that cycle of dependence which perpetuates itself from one illiterate generation to the next. If this should be the case, then for the first time in our modern history we may see the growth of a hereditary and illiterate underclass in the United States. To say that this would be a tragedy for our democracy would be a commonplace. To indicate how Congress may divine the means by which to fend off such a tragedy is far more useful; this I will attempt to do. . . .

What Should be Done?

The key ingredient in all of the best programs I have seen is a commitment to authentic, grass-roots neighborhood involvement. The term conventionally applied to programs rooted at the local level is "community-based." The term is easily misunderstood and just as easily mistrusted. The work "community" is equated, in the minds of some observers, with an adversarial or bellicose approach. This misconception warrants brief correction. Whether the initiating agency should be a library, a college, a national organization such as LVA or Laubach Literacy, or one of the thousands of small neighborhood programs financed by tiny hand-outs, backed by churches, staffed by low-paid organizers or by volunteers, the shared ingredient is one that stands right in the mainstream of American tradition.

What is it that is so important about programs of this kind?

They tend, first of all, to win the loyalty of people with the lowest reading levels who are seldom drawn to formal, institutionalized, and distant settings. They also tend to deal with reading problems in a broader context of the needs of children and of neighborhood regeneration. Their learners tend to have much better records of completion. Finally, these locally based programs tend to operate with minimal overhead, little bureaucracy, and therefore accomplish more at lower cost than other programs.

Illiterates have a difficult time overcoming their anxiety and terror of humiliation. Community programs overcome these fears in several ways:

(1) The programs are most often near the homes of those they serve. The fear of distance, or an unknown street, the fear of being lost amongst a maze of bus or subway signs one cannot read, is instantly diminished.

(2) The cost of travel and the loss of hours—two hours' transportation to receive an hour of instruction—are removed.

(3) Weather and other unpredictables (a child's illness, for example) cease to be deterrents when the program is across the street or down the block. In public housing projects, where there frequently are empty units, neighborhood programs can create a learning center in the buildings where the largest numbers of potential learners presently reside.

(4) Recruitment becomes infinitely simpler and far more human when initiated by a person who is known, as friend or neighbor, to those adults in the greatest need. The stranger with a clipboard who comes into a poor neighborhood is not likely to be trusted. Similar distrust accrues to the recruitment office in a distant public building. (Schools are particularly intimidating places for recruitment. They are the scene of childhood fear and former failure for illiterate adults.) A neighborhood center also has the opportunity to draw upon the insights of those people who already know which of their neighbors cannot read and who,

whether as volunteers or hired organizers, can provide the bridge between the learners and potential teachers.

"How do you reach them?" One poor woman in Ohio asked, then answered her own question: "You cannot do it by sitting downtown and mailing out brochures. You need to find the kind of person who can walk the neighborhood—someone with a heart and soul. A foot-walker. Someone like that would know very quickly who was illiterate and who was not. That person has got to be able to overcome the illiterate's terror of the outside world . . . Sojourner Truth said: 'I cannot read, but I can read people.' So, too, can many of the poorest people in their own communities."

An enlightened fiscal policy would profit from this good advice by hiring unemployed adults, taking them off welfare, and assigning them the dignity and income of engaged participants in what would be a most dramatic and authentic bootstrap operation.

(5) The learning process in itself becomes more optimistic when neighbors learn and study in small groups of six or eight, drawing strength from those around them, helping one another, and receiving reassurance that their difficulties are not unique but shared by those beside them.

(6) Instructors often are recruited from among the residents of neighborhoods like these. In neighborhoods where even as many as 40 percent of residents need literacy help, it is easy to forget that 60 percent remain as a potential pool of tutors. Programs like these will still need outside teachers and professional direction. But good instructors also will emerge out of the neighborhood itself. Some of the most effective and devoted teachers are precisely those who came as students some years earlier.

A young man named Fernando at a literacy center in San Francisco told me this: "I came in four years ago because I needed help to read and write. I still don't write as well as I'd like. But I know well enough to teach. So I'm teaching, but I'm learning still at the same time. One day they said they had a job for a part-time director. That's my job. I'm getting paid. It's not much money, but it pays the rent."

There are thousands of people like Fernando. Few have had the opportunity to give as well as to receive. Few community programs have the funds to channel decency and loyalty in such constructive ways. Financial incentives to make it possible for former learners to grow into teachers of their own communities would enhance the stirring character of neighborhood regeneration at its best. This, in turn, would help to cut down on the settlement house mentality which plagues even the finest literacy programs. "People don't like you to 'do' for them," one woman said. "They need to learn how they can do it for *themselves.*" This, again, seems at the very heart of bootstrap transformation in the mainstream of American tradition.

(7) Illiterate parents must provide for somebody to take care of their children while they learn to read and write. Daycare is provided with

51

the greatest ease in literacy programs close to home. Far more important, children of illiterate adults can be provided early-learning opportunities in the same locations where their parents learn to read. Adult literacy centers, in an optimal situation, ought to be attached to pre-school programs.

Much has been said of "job-related literacy." While not disparaging one jot of value of this emphasis, I will suggest another concept here. I call it "child-centered literacy"—a literacy that draws upon the deepest motivation that most parents know: the love for their own child. The two motivations (work opportunities and parental love) should not be regarded as if they were mutually exclusive. In community programs, both can be incorporated in a single stroke.

(8) Where parents do not need or are not able to participate in literacy work, it is frequently grandparents (or another relative, an older sibling for example) who may join in child/adult programs. When grandparents are involved in the same programs as grandchildren, certain possibilities of story-telling by the very old to those who are the very young begin to summon up some of the most exciting memories of our American colonial tradition. Story-telling is, of course, a Biblical tradition too. Experts have some complicated theories about "adult motivation." I believe that love is the most potent motivation in our souls. Wise government policy, tending towards a Family Literacy concept, might enable us to draw upon the longing of the old to share their memories and heritage with those they love the most.

(9) Finally, a neighborhood literacy focus helps to guarantee that those who learn will do so in a spirit of collaboration and of shared concerns. Institutional programs built exclusively upon the individual and economic aspiration of the learner tend to foster the desire to escape one's neighborhood and move into a separate realm of life. The consequence is something like a "brain-drain" on those neighborhoods which can't afford to lose their most successful residents. Community programs, by recycling successful learners into organizers, teachers, and recruiters, help to build more closely knit, more prosperous, and less dependent populations.

Specific Recommendations

This committee will by now have heard advice from other witnesses with a variety of specialized approaches—job-related, military, volunteer, and private sector—all of which command attention. It is important to add one caveat, however. All of these programs now exist and all together serve at most two million, or approximately three or four percent, of those in need. If such approaches alone had been sufficient, we would not be meeting here today.

In arguing for community-based child/adult action, I am proposing something new and something which offers us the opportunity to rescue those who are adults from present suffering and to help prevent the likelihood that we shall see another generation of illiterate Americans leaving public schools two decades hence. These are some specific actions which I urge you to consider:

(1) Congress might discover methods to expand the Head Start concept to a Family Literacy concept. Parents, older siblings, and grandparents lacking literacy skills might be recruited, through this plan, to learn both for their own sake and to reinforce the early education of the young.

(2) Congress might assure that public housing projects built with federal funds provide space for establishment of Family Learning Centers, sparing organizers in this way the cost of rental, heat, and upkeep for a literacy program. These are precisely the kinds of trivial costs which sometimes occupy about one half the time of organizers in the best (and always underfunded) local programs.

(3) Congress might explore the means of implementing the two previous suggestions in a number of demonstration models. These might be adapted from existing programs which already have established strong community support. In other instances, such a demonstration model might well be developed as the cornerstone of a high-energy project which is just now moving into operation.

(4) Congress might assist in breaking down the incorrect impression that volunteers alone can meet the problem. This is not to underestimate the volunteer potential in American society. (Retired persons, to give only one example, are a natural and rich resource that we have foolishly neglected.) But volunteers cannot be trained, assigned, and supervised—nor can they find the neighborhood allies, the "footwalkers" I've described—without skilled, stable, and paid staff. The choice is not between the federal dollar and the local volunteer potential.

In the interest of bipartisan consensus, I will refrain for a change from recommending vast expenditures. It seems only honest to say just this much: While it is clear that we can never be assured of getting what we pay for, it is certain we will never get what we *do not* pay for. With over $100 billion lost each year because of the dependent status of America's illiterates, it would seem self-evident that any investment in the demonstration projects I have recommended would be returned to us in unimagined savings. It is unusual to find an issue where the claims of civic decency so closely coincide with the most clear-cut economic interests of our nation. Federal support for local literacy action may well represent the one good cause on which conservatives and liberals, rich and poor, the business-minded and the socially committed may wholeheartedly agree.

One approach which might make sense to Congress is the possible establishment of a "Literacy Service Corps." For young and literate adults, such a program might become a national alternative to military service; it would be unfortunate, however, if such a corps were to be limited exclusively to young people. Older persons, as we have seen—especially retired people—ought to be encouraged to take part. On the basis of 20 years' experience in organizing volunteers, I am confident that the response would be spectacular.

Congress might consider whether such a literacy corps might be incorporated into an expanded VISTA (Volunteers in Service to America) organization or developed as a separate program altogether.

(5) Finally, serious thinking should be given to the hiring of literate people who live in those neighborhoods of high illiteracy in order to enable them to serve as the recruitment arm and, wherever possible, part of the teaching force for the instruction of their neighbors. People who are willing to participate in work as difficult as this ought to be given high incentive to remove themselves from welfare programs and to form part of a bootstrap effort that will reinforce our economic and political well-being.

I have in mind a woman whom I interviewed in Cleveland, a very poor but undefeated woman who was living in a public housing project. I asked this woman, barely literate herself, whether there was something she could do to help those of her friends who could not read or write at all. "What could I do? I could sit down every night and teach them right here in this kitchen. Just give me help. Just show me what to do. And tell me what day we begin!"

Her voice tells us of enormous energy and decency untapped and wasted in American society. There are thousands of us at the grassroots level who can help to show her what to do. But only Congress can tell her, and can tell America, on what day we begin.

DEALING WITH ILLITERACY

ILLITERACY CAMPAIGNS
ARE MISGUIDED

Thomas G. Sticht

Thomas G. Sticht is the president of Applied Behavioral and Cognitive Sciences, Inc. and adjunct research professor of the United States Naval Postgraduate School.

Points to Consider:

1. What does the author mean by the term "intergenerational illiteracy"?
2. Why does the author disagree with Jonathan Kozol's definition that "35 million adults reading in the 6th to 8th grade range should be considered '. . . illiterate in terms of U.S. print communications at the present time.' "?
3. How do adult literacy programs improve the education of both parents and children?
4. What does the author offer as an alternative to the "war on illiteracy"?

Excerpted from testimony of Thomas G. Sticht before the House Sub-committee on Elementary, Secondary, and Vocational Education of the House Committee on Education and Labor, October 1, 1985.

Unfortunately, it seems to me, no matter how well intentioned, calls for a "war" or "campaign" against illiteracy are misleading and distract from very serious problems of adult education.

The "Illiteracy" Problem[a]

Periodically, the problem of adult "illiteracy" is discovered in the United States. This cyclical phenomenon has been thoughtfully documented by Dr. Wanda Cook in a book published and distributed by the International Reading Association. She notes that from time to time, usually in association with some major social disturbance, such as World Wars I and II, the civil rights movement during the 1960s, and periods of economic unrest, it is noted that millions of adults cannot read and write, or that they do so only with minimal skills. During these cycles of awareness of adult literacy problems, there are frequently calls for "campaigns" to "stamp out illiteracy" once and for all. Most recently, Mr. Jonathan Kozol, in his book titled *Illiterate America* (Doubleday, 1985), asserts that some 60 million U.S. adults should be called ". . . illiterate in terms of U.S. print communications at the present time.", and he then goes on to call, once again, for ". . . an all out literacy war in the United States." at a cost of some $10 billion.

Unfortunately, it seems to me, no matter how well intentioned, such calls for a "war" or "campaign" against illiteracy are misleading and distract from very serious problems of adult education. These problems result in large part from the fact that, on the one hand, literacy must be developed anew in each new generation and this process too often goes poorly in the case of the children of undereducated adults and, on the other hand, the problem of "intergenerational illiteracy" is exacerbated by the fact that the "levels" of literacy needed to function well in our society are not fixed in either their nature or extent and so today's "literate" may be tomorrow's "illiterate." Neither of these conditions of contemporary U.S. education are addressed by "quick-fix" "campaigns" to "stamp-out illiteracy." Rather, they demand institutional changes in both our attitudes toward adult education and in our commitment to provide opportunities for lifelong adult education and training.

---

[a]These comments are an extension of comments that appeared in an editorial in the *Wall Street Journal* of September 3, 1985.

"Intergenerational Illiteracy"

The recurrent nature of adult literacy problems is demonstrated by the fact that each year many students enter our public schools who come from homes in which they have been unable to acquire the minimal competencies needed to succeed in school; many of these students later become dropouts and failures of the school system; they then become the unemployed, lower socioeconomic status, marginally literate parents of a new generation of students who, in their turn, will enter the schools without the minimum competencies needed to succeed, and the cycle of marginal literacy and marginal living repeats itself again and again.

Current attempts to break the cycles of marginal literacy and marginal living focus resources on compensatory education programs operated in the public schools, where it is hoped that the disadvantages of the home can be overcome by dint of extra effort at school. Recently, this extra effort amounted to some $3.48 billion in Title I funding (fiscal year 1984).

When it is discovered from time to time, as it has been today, that, despite the billions of dollars of compensatory education, millions of young people have dropped out of or graduated from high school with reading skills below the fifth grade level, or the currently perceived level of literacy thought necessary for adequately functioning in our society, additional efforts may be made to provide education to out-of-school youth and adults. However, these efforts take on quite a different character from the compensatory programs in the public schools. Most noticeable is the difference in the amount of federal funding for adult basic education, which this year amounted to around $100 million, less than 3 percent of the Title I funds. Furthermore, rather than providing for thousands of professionally trained adult educators, as is done in the case of special education teachers for children, it is expected that adult basic education programs can be mostly staffed with volunteers, as in the current National Adult Literacy Initiative, and that they will be

57

Reprinted by permission: Tribune Media Services.

of limited duration, fast-acting, far-reaching, and bring about not only sizeable increases in academic literacy skills, but also improvement in gaining employment, parenting, community participation, and a host of other things.

The Changing Nature of "Literacy"

Compounding the problems of "intergenerational illiteracy" is the fact that the standards for being recognized as "literate" in contemporary society have risen dramatically in the last fifty years (see Figure I). Problems facing the schools as they attempt to ensure the achievement of rising standards of literacy by each child, are magnified by the need to provide education to an ever increasing diversity of learning aptitude, cultural and language backgrounds. In 1980, for instance, the public schools enrolled 3.3 million handicapped students, II million members of various racial or ethnic groups, and some I million students of limited English proficiency (U.S. Department of Education, 1982).

The diversity of student backgrounds, coupled with the need to have each child reach ever higher levels of literacy strains the capacity of the traditional school system, and the traditional job of the teacher. In earlier times, schools handled the problem of diversity by screening out a significant part of the population (for example, blacks, rural farm children, and the learning disabled were permitted to avoid school or to drop out in the elementary grades) and by permitting a wide range

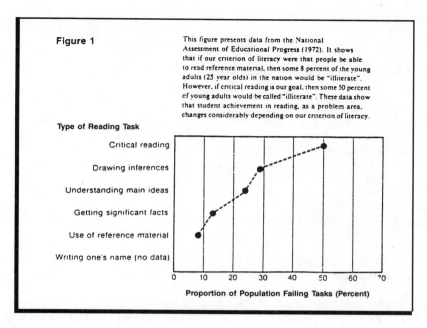

Figure 1

This figure presents data from the National Assessment of Educational Progress (1972). It shows that if our criterion of literacy were that people be able to read reference material, then some 8 percent of the young adults (25 year olds) in the nation would be "illiterate". However, if critical reading is our goal, then some 50 percent of young adults would be called "illiterate". These data show that student achievement in reading, as a problem area, changes considerably depending on our criterion of literacy.

Type of Reading Task

Critical reading

Drawing inferences

Understanding main ideas

Getting significant facts

Use of reference material

Writing one's name (no data)

0   10   20   30   40   50   60   70

Proportion of Population Failing Tasks (Percent)

U.S House of Representatives Committee on Education and Labor.

of achievement, resulting in many high school graduates with less than ninth grade literacy abilities. While generally acceptable as a level of achievement a generation or so ago, youth and adults with sixth to ninth grade literacy skills are today considered as "functionally illiterate" or as "illiterate." For instance, in developing the foundations for his call for a "literacy war" in the United States, Mr. Kozol argues that some 35 million adults reading in the sixth to eighth grade range should be considered ". . . illiterate in terms of U.S. print communications at the present time."

But here, it seems to me, we run the risk of trivializing the problems of undereducated adults by referring to them as "illiterates." Clearly, people who can read with the knowledge and skills demanded by the fifth through eighth grades are not illiterate. In fact, in February of this year I taught a reading skills program for young adults, some of whom read in the sixth to ninth grade range, and found that they could perform a great number of reading tasks, though they frequently had problems with spelling and analytical thought. But they were not "illiterate." They, like millions of other youth and adults, can benefit from a lot more serious, rigorous education and training in many areas of knowledge. And they can use their "middle range" literacy skills to gain new knowledge by reading, writing, analyzing, computing, graphing, reporting, and interacting with knowledgeable teachers and peers. What they cannot benefit much from is the "phonics," "decoding," "word attack," and light reading that is offered in the 50 or so hours of tutoring that most "illiterates" get in voluntary literacy "campaigns."

Finding Solutions to Adult Literacy Problems

If we are to find solutions to problems of adult "illiteracy" in the United States, we need to first come to an appreciation of the ramifications of the two factors affecting education discussed above. These are (1) each new generation of "illiterate" infants must be educated to high levels of literacy, and particular problems are posed by the children of undereducated adults; and (2) the nature and extent of literacy needed to function well are not fixed.

Regarding the first factor, we must recognize that both the education of parents and their children is needed if children are to enter the school system with the competencies and attitudes needed to succeed. From this point of view, adult literacy programs should be regarded as compensatory education for the adult's children. Elsewhere I have reviewed a growing body of evidence to suggest that the benefits of adult education most usually transfer to the education of their offspring (paper for the National Academy of Education, Human Resources Research Organization, Professional Paper 2.83, February 1983; see also World Bank Reprint Series Number 247, paper by Nancy Birdsall and Susan Hill Cochrane, 1982 for international evidence of the effects of parental education on the subsequent educational achievement of their children). Perhaps the most dramatic demonstration of the effects of parent education on the subsequent educational achievement of their children in the U.S. occurred after World War II when veterans who used the GI Bill to further their own education were found to have children who went further in school.

Thus, investment in programs for adult literacy development may produce "double duty dollars," because by improving the education of the adults, we may improve the educability of their children.

Regarding the second factor, by increasing our commitment to adult education, we should, over time, be better able to cope with the problems posed by changing literacy requirements. If adult education improves the educability of children, then the schools should be able to do a better job of bringing more jobs to higher levels of achievement without the need for extensive, compensatory education programs for preschool and elementary school children. Additionally, we provide a means to permit adults of all educational levels to achieve their education goals, whether these be personal or vocational. And of special importance to national economic and security interests, arrangements will be in place for retraining and upgrading the skills of those displaced by technology or international economic changes.

With concern for adult literacy development currently at a high level among community groups, business, and government policy makers, the challenge now is to avoid the "quick-fix," "war on illiteracy," "campaign" mentality that has plagued the field of adult basic education for decades. This does not mean that good works underway should stop. Rather, it means that, as current efforts progress, planning should be underway to put in place what is currently missing in the United States, that is, a comprehensive policy and system for human resources development that recognizes the need for both childhood and adulthood opportunities for sound education.

While it is difficult for me to conceive of what all might be entailed by a committment to a total human resources development policy, this will have to be determined by a national commission or other appropriate forum after considerable thought, we can anticipate that, if this policy links children's and adults' literacy development that there should be some overall cost savings in compensatory education programs. Further, if programs conducted by the Department of Defense, Labor, Agriculture, and Education could be, if not consolidated, then at least coordinated, additional adult education benefits might be secured without too much additional cost.

For instance, if the Department of Defense agreed to accept up to 20 percent of its enlisted force from those young adults now excluded because of education deficiencies, and to educate and train them as they have repeatedly done in the past, then those young people would receive education while in the military and they would also qualify for the new GI Bill, and, presumably, their children would benefit through the "intergenerational transfer" of education. The latter could be monitored by the Department of Education.

Additional benefits could be achieved by recognizing that "literacy" is not something different from education or training. Rather, literacy is developed by engaging students in the use of written tests and in writing. More attention of such activities in the context of job training in the Job Corps or programs conducted by the Job Training and Partnership Act could pay dividends in developing both job skills and literacy skills.

In short, better use of compensatory education funds, educational opportunities provided by military, labor, community colleges, "correctional" facilities, industry, and other existing adult education and training providers, coupled with better prepared educators from rejuvenated professional schools of education, and some funds for needed research, could go a long way to providing a more cost-effective education system for "stamping-in" literacy in each new generation, and for meeting the requirements of lifelong learning in the wake of inevitable cultural change.

9   DEALING WITH ILLITERACY

IMPROVING PERFORMANCE WILL NOT BE COST FREE

John C. Manning

John C. Manning, Ph.D., is a Professor of Education at the University of Minnesota. He is also president of the International Reading Association, a professional society of over 60,000 members and 1,180 affiliate councils in 36 nations interested in reading, reading education, and the promotion of literacy.

Points to Consider:

1. How did national policy makers view reading during the 1960s? 1970s?
2. What are the costs of illiteracy to society?
3. If students are not eligible to receive special programming under Chapter 1, where do they go to learn how to read? What usually happens to these students?
4. Since full funding of existing programs is unlikely to occur, what recommendations does the author make to the federal government?

Excerpted from testimony of John C. Manning before the House Subcommittee on Elementary, Secondary, and Vocational Education of the House Committee on Education and Labor, August 1, 1985.

There is a national responsibility to create the opportunity for all citizens to acquire those literacy skills necessary to ensure not only their own productivity but that of the next generation as well.

Illiteracy is a problem of national scope, a problem which affects every citizen in very concrete ways. It is a problem involving people and their productivity, their education, their intellectual fulfillment, their health, and their safety. In a very real sense, it is an issue bearing on the very security of our nation. It is, furthermore, a complex problem which will not yield to simplistic solutions. Only sustained efforts at many levels—national, state, local, and individual—will result in higher levels of literacy for all.

Introduction

Estimates of the magnitude of illiteracy in this land vary considerably. Most researchers agree that illiteracy affects millions of adult Americans. Figures approximating 10 percent of the adult population are commonly cited. These figures vary depending on the specific definition of illiteracy being used at the time. Functional illiteracy has usually been described as existing when an individual has completed fewer than eight years of schooling and does not have the ability to complete everyday reading activities with a minimal degree of ease and accuracy.

It is also difficult to make comparisons between the illiteracy rate now and that of previous years, since the demands on readers have increased considerably as the society has increased in technological sophistication. What was sufficient reading ability in past decades does not serve today's reader well as he or she seeks to make a contribution in an increasingly complex society. What is agreed upon by everyone is that adult illiteracy is a very substantial problem affecting large numbers of individuals in every segment of our society.

Related to the difficulty of reaching consensus on definitions of illiteracy are similar difficulties in the delineation of clear national goals in this area. During the 1960s, reading was viewed by national policy makers as a right (as in the federally sponsored "Right to Read" program) whereas in the 1970s it was viewed more from the perspective of a skill (as exemplified by the emphasis on basic skills and functional literacy). Recent national reports have reinforced the impression that young adults have not learned to read well enough and that, as a nation, we need to do something about the situation. This problem of goals and definitions may have been a hindrance to the development and implementation of a coherent and effective national effort. . . .

63

BETTER SCHOOLS

Better schools will take more money, and some of it should come from the federal government.

USA Today, *December 14, 1983*

Definitions and Statistics

Definitions of literacy and estimates of the magnitude of the problem vary greatly, according to the source referred to. Depending on which statistic you read, you might believe that illiteracy is out of control or that it is a problem of much smaller magnitude. For example, one commonly used definition of literacy has been the ability to read at about the fourth grade level. In 1900, acccording to the definition then used by the U.S. Bureau of the Census, the illiteracy rate in the United States was 11.3 percent of the adult population. By 1980, using the same definition, the rate would be 0.5 percent of the adult population. However, standards have changed and a higher level of reading skill is essential even to function minimally in our present society.

Northcutt reported in the Adult Performance Level (APL) study (1975) that 23 million adult Americans were functionally illiterate. His work defined literacy as being the application of communications, computation, problem-solving, and interpersonal relations skills to the general areas of occupational knowledge, consumer economics, community resources, government and law, and health.

Donald Fisher, in a 1978 study of functional literacy funded by the National Institute of Education, concluded that low estimates of illiteracy (under 10 percent) were found as frequently as higher estimates.

A discussion of the statistics must also include the fact that illiteracy rates are not equal in all segments of our society. Hispanic Americans, Native Americans, and black Americans all have rates of illiteracy higher than the national average. Using the older definition of the Bureau of the Census, in 1980 white American illiteracy could be determined to be 0.4 percent, black American illiteracy to be 1.6 percent.

In contrast, using different definitions, the APL study found that 56 percent of the Hispanic Americans and 47 percent of the black Americans were functionally illiterate, as compared to 16 percent of white Americans. With respect to non-English speaking individuals in the country, many of them are illiterate not only in English, but also in their primary language.

This situation creates a massive problem for teaching literacy skills to these individuals. In a recent study funded by the National Institute

64

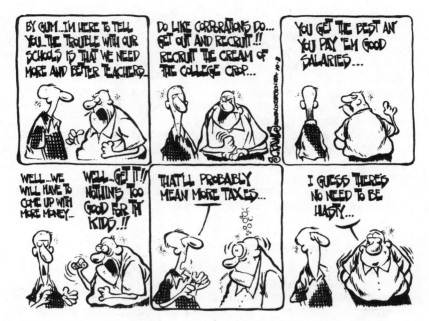

of Education (Reder, 1983), a study of non-English speaking immigrants found that individuals who were literate in their primary language acquired English literacy skills at a faster rate than their non-literate counterparts.

Another special population, handicapped Americans, has a higher than average rate of illiteracy. This population includes learning disabled adults who have perceptual problems which create massive barriers to learning to read.

In short, illiteracy has been shown to be a problem of significant magnitude. Definitions and estimates may vary but the importance of the issue is agreed to by all.

Costs to Society

The costs of illiteracy to society are massive. On Sri Lanka, the tiny republic off the southeastern tip of India, waterborne diseases crippled thousands of people. In program after program, they tried to teach the families to cover their water pots while cooking their food. They all failed. However, once the people were taught to read, they changed their orientation toward health and hygiene. Waterborne diseases were no longer rampant.

Within the U.S., the report *A Nation at Risk* (1983) stated that: "Business and military leaders complain that they are required to spend millions of dollars on costly remedial education and training programs in such basic skills as reading, writing, spelling, and computation."

In this country, an adult illiterate is a lost resource. The individual has trouble reading subway signs, tax forms, children's report cards, and consumer information.

An obvious result of illiteracy is unemployment. Illiterates in a recent study were found to be unable to find their way to a job interview without a great deal of assistance. While trying to remember the address, they had to find their way around the city by attempting to read street signs, bus and subway inside a building, using wall maps, and asking directions. Once there, they had to fill out a job application form. It is not surprising, then, that adult illiterates frequently do not even try to find their way out of the patterns they have come to depend upon in order to live and survive. In a nation that prides itself on individualism, the potential of these individuals is lost to society, to their families, and to themselves.

Instructional Approaches

Models of adult basic education and literacy programs vary. Generally speaking, adult illiterates are taught how to read in community-based programs, library-based programs, industry-based programs, and government-based programs. Each has one thing in common—there is a teacher who cares. Skilled teachers use a variety of instructional approaches. Most incorporate phonics into their teaching. Some programs are computer or technology based. Effective reading instruction has always been characterized by two important factors: (1) the teacher has a method and knows how to use it, and (2) the learner wants to learn.

The adult as a learner is different than the child as a learner. Adult learners bring to the learning environment a broader background of life experience, a sense of why they are participating, specific expectations and goals, and a personal sense of past academic accomplishments. Some educators have described the teaching of an adult learner as being as much personalized counseling as it is academic instruction. Much is still unknown about the adult learner. The federal government should be funding research on reading for the adult learner.

Federal Response

Around the world, national responses to illiteracy have usually followed one of two models. The first approach has been to institute a national mass literacy effort. The other model is a community-based approach. In a 1984 UNESCO (United Nation's Educational Scientific and Cultural Organization) synthesis by Bola, 15 national mass literacy campaigns were studied. In all programs, the major focus was to raise the entire nation's literacy level. These mass literacy efforts often proved to be short-lived. The second approach, to work on a national movement to build literacy programs in each community and to link resources to economic development, has gained favor by many observers in the United States (Hunter and Harman, 1979).

Basically, the United States has no national policy. Currently, the Administration is funding the Adult Literacy Initiative, which is working with the national Coalition for Literacy and the Advertising Council to produce public service announcements designed to build a wider awareness of the illiteracy problem and to enlist volunteer tutors and corporate support. The Adult Literacy Initiative is also encouraging the development of state and local literacy councils. The Department of Education is also funding the National Assessment of Young Adults through the National Assessment of Educational Progress (NAEP) program. This study may provide a clearer assessment of the extent of the illiteracy problem. All of these efforts are useful and important. But they are not enough.

Paul Delker, the Department of Education official in charge of the Adult Education program, has reported that each year more students enter the category of adult illiterates by leaving school without the ability to read. There are several reasons for this situation.

Only one half of the students eligible to receive special programming under Chapter I of the Education Consolidation and Improvement Act are funded to participate in the remedial reading and mathematics programs offered to disadvantaged students. Where do the rest go to learn how to read?

Many students who cannot read are labeled handicapped by the schools and are sent to special classes for the learning disabled. These classes are usually taught by teachers without training in the teaching of reading. What happens to them? Since the major presenting symptom of learning disability is usually a reading problem, it seems reasonable to require that the learning disabilities and special education teacher be trained in the teaching of reading.

Many high risk students such as these, without effective reading instruction, eventually become part of the adult illiteracy statistics.

Some adults who want to learn how to read well enough to meet a personal goal find instruction through the community-based services of the Laubach or Literacy Volunteers programs. Others receive help on the job. Still others find help at tutoring programs conducted by their local libraries. But most who find programs find them as part of the adult basic education program. However, all of these sources of knowledge are blocked to many adults because of problems associated with schedules, transportation, or child care or simply because of lack of room in the programs.

What else can be done? A massive spending program aimed at fully funding the elementary and secondary education programs now on the books would make a difference. But full funding is unlikely to occur. Fully developing a set of community-based programs linked with

67

the Adult Education programs of the states could work, but that too is unlikely to occur.

Specific Recommendations

What then can be done with limited resources? The federal government could take a much more active role in the fight to reduce adult illiteracy by:

1. Increasing educational research in areas of adult learning, adult illiteracy, and the instruction of adults;
2. Promoting the development of teacher education and certification programs for teachers of adult learners;
3. Promoting the development of new learning materials for the adult learner, including computer-based materials;
4. Encouraging the development of programs to coordinate the many community-based, adult basic education programs and non-traditional education programs;
5. Promoting the development of television-based education programs either through the cable-dedicated channels or microwave mediums;
6. Rewarding employers who train adult illiterates to become literate and productive workers; and
7. Coordinating the federal government's education, health and human services, defense, agriculture, and labor programs that affect the illiterate adult.

Literacy demands are increasing for almost every job in the country. Tom Sticht's* work with the reading requirements of various occupational categories of the Army determined that functioning as a soldier required measurable literacy skills. A military policeman needed to be able to read on the eleventh grade level and an infantryman on the tenth grade level. Just since World War II, the literacy levels required by the military have increased. Literacy is not a static notion. To arrive at a definition of literacy, one must take into consideration both the skill level of the individual and the demands of the world around him.

Literacy is vitally important in the workplace and for the continued growth of our economy. Literate workers can adapt and change. Illiterate workers must depend on developed patterns in order to cope. The country needs workers who can adapt and change with the changing economy. There is a national responsibility to create the opportunity for all citizens to acquire those literacy skills necessary to ensure not only their own productivity but that of the next generation as well.

---

*Editor's note: Tom Sticht's biography appears on page 55 of Reading 8.

10 DEALING WITH ILLITERACY

INSPIRED EFFORT AND DISCIPLINE, NOT MORE MONEY, IS THE ANSWER

William J. Bennett

William J. Bennett is the Secretary of Education. Under his direction, the Department of Education has sought to provide the American people with the most reliable and practical information on what works in educating children. This reading is adapted from the third book in the Department of Education's "What Works" series.

Points to Consider:

1. The author notes that many students from poor areas of several major U.S. cities are performing at or above grade level in reading and math. What principles have these schools used to be successful?
2. Why is education described as a powerful instrument?
3. Instead of increased spending, what does the author suggest as the single greatest need for improvement?
4. How can the federal government help in the education of disadvantaged children?

U.S. Department of Education, *Schools That Work: Educating Disadvantaged Children.* Washington, D.C.: U.S. Government Printing Office, 1987.

Too often we have spent money on the wrong things and have not achieved good results. The success of many schools springs from a focus on sound principles, not higher expenditures.

Americans have always believed that good schools make a difference. Our faith is that a good education can help children overcome even the most severe effects of poverty, and can provide our children with the traits of character and the shared knowledge and beliefs necesary for personal and economic success. . . .

Schools that Succeed

As Secretary of Education I have visited more than 70 schools throughout every part of the United States. Among them have been good schools in the poorest areas of Dallas, Cleveland, Chicago, Washington, D.C., Boston, Phoenix, and New York. These are schools that give their students what a good school must: a respect for and interest in learning and the habits and motivation necessary for success and achievement. Few students drop out of these schools. Most perform at or above grade level in reading and math; many go on to college. In these schools, children's family circumstances and their parents' lack of income or education do not hold them back.

The success of such schools is not a miracle. It is not a mystery. It is accomplished through the inspired effort of committed adults who adhere strictly to certain bedrock principles and sternly refuse to succumb to defeatism. Let us consider these principles.

Every Child is Important

First, these schools hold to the traditional American view that no immutable law dooms a child to failure simply because he or she is born into poverty. The principals and staff of these schools believe they *can* make a difference. They do not look at students and see broad socioeconomic categories. They see children. And they focus on those children, help get them on their feet, and point them the way up. Parents can be a great help in this effort, and many successful schools have enlisted help from disadvantaged parents. But disadvantaged parents, like all parents, vary in the degree to which they take an interest in their children's education. Nevertheless, when parents do not take an active interest, good schools do not take this as an excuse for failing to educate children.

It is not unusual for principals in these schools to know the name of every student. And in every one of these schools the administration and faculty make an effort to get responsible adults from throughout

70

the community involved in the enterprise of education. This community of adults makes clear to disadvantaged students that, no matter who they are or where they come from, they can learn.

Clear Communication

Second, these schools help children develop the qualities of character and respect for the principles of right and wrong that are prized by American society at large. The adults in these schools understand that the ideals and knowledge they must communicate remain the same whether the students are rich or poor, black or white. Such schools do not deny or neglect differences in background and preparation; their students may be given even more structure, more homework, and more individual attention by teachers than students in other schools. And these students are not measured against lower standards. Their teachers know that disadvantaged students learn best when they are offered the best: clear standards of behavior, a curriculum that is rich and challenging, and vigorous teaching.

"Old-fashioned" Fundamentals

Finally, these good schools do not trade fundamentals for novelty, and they tend to avoid what is not tried and true. These schools are not disheartened by a history of low student performance, poor teaching skills or high suspension rates. Instead they are inspired to act. They respond with more homework, better teachers, longer hours, tougher discipline, harder work, and greater encouragement to achieve. They set goals for students in precise and measurable terms. They teach the basics—reading, mathematics, science, writing—and communicate the essentials of an American common culture: history, literature, patriotism, and democratic principles. In other words, they provide an "intellectual work ethic" in what some people might disparagingly call "the old-fashioned way." And it works.

71

What Works

SCHOOLS THAT WORK

Educating Disadvantaged Children

U.S. Department of Education

The Department of Education, under Secretary Bennet, has sought to provide the American people with practical information regarding the education of children in its *What Works* series.

72

Education: A Powerful Instrument

An ever-expanding body of social science research confirms that our faith in education is not misplaced. School has proven to be the single best avenue out of poverty, and educational achievement is now the most accurate predictor of a person's future economic success.

The United States, where schooling is the most powerful instrument of social mobility, deserves high marks for extending educational opportunities to all our citizens. We have spent generously for education, particularly for disadvantaged children. But expanded spending and access to education mean little if the quality of that education in a particular school is poor. Too many schools serving disadvantaged children are characterized by low test scores, poor achievement, lax discipline, and an inability to retain and graduate their students.

A Focus on Sound Principles

The notion that poverty and bad schools are inevitably linked is a prescription for inaction. It is a self-fulfilling prophecy of despair and it is flat-out wrong. Americans should not accept excuses for educational failure. Some of the reforms we need may, in some circumstances, require increased spending, but most will not. Too often we have spent money on the wrong things and have not achieved good results. The success of many schools springs from a focus on sound principles, not higher expenditures. . . .

In many disadvantaged communities, real improvement will take some doing. Schools may need more help, specialized instruction, improved textbooks, better teachers, and higher standards for graduation and promotion. Principals may need the administrative autonomy and authority to hire unusually qualified teachers with unconventional backgrounds, and to offer them the performance incentives that will get them to stay if they are successful and get them to leave if they are not. Parents may need to demand that information about the overall performance of their children's school be collected and publicized so that they can judge how well it is performing and, if necessary, choose another local school better suited to their children's needs. And in many places, the single greatest need may be for a principal or teacher of a certain character who combines the qualities of a greater leader and a modest hero....

In summary—

- Children from all backgrounds can learn, if they are given the proper opportunity and encouragement.
- Equity and high standards go hand in hand. We will have equity for disadvantaged children only when they are offered a high quality education.
- We know how to create successful schools for the disadvantaged. It takes commitment, hard work, and imagination; but it can be done.
- Schools must be given the freedom to design the best possible programs for their students, while being held accountable for their performance.
- Parents—regardless of their income level or formal education—can help improve their children's achievement in school.

Principals can—

- Inspire their students with a vision of excellence and develop practical plans for realizing this vision.
- Communicate their vision to everyone involved with the school—students, parents, school staff, and community members.
- Create a safe and orderly school environment that is conducive to learning. School goals must include standards for behavior as well as academic progress.
- Build and retain a talented staff that is committed to teaching all the children.

Teachers and school administrators can—

- Help instill the values and attitudes their students need for success in school and beyond. Schools must nurture a love of learning, a belief that hard work and persistence pay off, and the habits of good citizenship.
- Provide a challenging academic curriculum. Disadvantaged students need the best that school can offer. The subject matter they study should be coherent and interesting and enable them to develop the thinking and analytic skills they will need in later life.
- Employ a variety of techniques within the classroom to structure learning, reward progress, and move students on to independent work.
- Provide language—minority students whose English proficiency is limited with the special help they need to achieve English fluency.
- Give disadvantaged students a good start by getting the parents of young children involved in educational programs or by including disadvantaged children in preschool programs.

74

- Reach out to parents to help them take part in educating their children. Make them partners with the school by keeping them informed of the schools' expectations and by making school personnel accessible to them.

Parents and guardians can—

- Instill in children the values they need to do well in school and throughout life. From the example they set, the stories they tell, and the way in which they speak to children, parents convey values. These values should prepare children to work hard in school and to keep up with their studies.
- Demand the best from their children and show they care by supervising their behavior. Parents can help their children learn by regulating leisure time and the amount of television watched and by encouraging children to read, converse, and keep up with their studies.
- Become involved with the schools. Parents must take responsibility for seeing whether the schools are expecting the most from their children and finding out how they can help the schools. The volunteer assistance of parents can go a long way toward increasing the effectiveness of schools.

Community groups must recognize their state in educating disadvantaged children by investing in their education and future success. Community school partnerships, incentive programs, and many other activities will make a difference for these children.

State and district education officials can—

- Ensure that education reforms make a difference in the education of disadvantaged children. This includes setting high standards in schools that serve the disadvantaged and making sure that special help is available to meet student needs.
- Get the right principal. The right man or woman can change a poor school into a good school and can make a good school a great school. Without the right person—one with energy, vision, commitment, and compassion—there is no enterprise. A struggling school in a poor community requires a leader who believes success is possible and can make others believe it too.
- Develop policies that are tightly structured with respect to results and loose structured with respect to means. Set high standards and demand accountability, but also offer schools the freedom to meet the needs of their students.
- Develop incentive programs that recognize exemplary schools and provide local units with discretionary funds for implementing long-term improvements.

- Provide parents with a choice in selecting their children's public schools by means of magnet schools and other arrangements.
- Publicize information on school performance, including such data as standardized test scores, graduation and attendance rates, course enrollments, awards, and population characteristics. Publishing school-by-school profiles help make schools accountable to the taxpayers.
- Use statewide testing to identify low-performing schools, set goals for their improvement, and target them for special assistance. When a school or district shows an inability to improve, take action to change leadership or even assume control.

State and local personnel bear the primary responsibility for education, but the federal government also plays a significant role in educating disadvantaged children. **The federal government should—**

- Continue to provide resources through programs such as compensatory education and education for students with limited English proficiency.
- Enact legislation that holds the schools accountable for spending federal funds effectively and for achieving results.
- Continue to make available the results of research for use by school personnel and the general public.
- Offer reliable information to groups and individuals who work to improve education for disadvantaged children.

11 DEALING WITH ILLITERACY

PHONICS IS THE ANSWER

Martha C. Brown

Martha C. Brown is a former high school and college teacher, with over 25 years experience. She is also an education writer and author of Schoolwise, *a handbook to help parents deal with children's school problems.*

Points to Consider:

1. How many children are reading one or more years below grade level? How many are reading two or more years below grade level?
2. What are the differences between direct phonics and indirect phonics?
3. Which method is considered more effective in teaching children how to read?
4. How many schools use direct phonics? How many use indirect phonics?

Excerpted from testimony of Martha C. Brown before the House Sub-committee on Elementary, Secondary, and Vocational Education of the House Committee on Education and Labor, March 20, 1986.

It is far easier and less expensive to teach children to read correctly in the first place than it is to remedy the problem by teaching illiterate adults after they have experienced the frustration of trying to function without reading skills in our society.

As a former high school and college teacher, as a parent, and as an education writer, I have been a close observer of our public schools for more than 25 years. Research for my recent book *Schoolwise*, a handbook to help parents deal with children's school problems, put me in touch with scores of parents, teachers, administrators, and education researchers across the United States.

I am pleased that the Congress is conducting hearings on the problem of illiteracy, which results in a life of frustration for a growing number of adults in this nation. The one third of our adult population which is totally or functionally illiterate is more likely to need welfare and more likely to be involved in crime than are adults who can read. Because we have compulsory schooling, the vast majority of our adult illiterates have spent at least eight years in the classroom. A large number have high school diplomas. Illiteracy is therefore an educational problem before it becomes a social problem. While I agree that we must make every effort to help adult illiterates learn to read, it is also essential that we find out why the illiterate adults who now need our help were not taught to read in school.

Lack of money is not the answer. We lead the developed nations in the proportion of our national resources devoted to education, as well as in the proportion of adult illiterates in our society. Two million illiterate young adults emerge from our schools each year.

Reading: The Number One Problem

Reading is the number one problem in U.S. education today—at all levels of schooling and in all types of communities. An untold number of children leave elementary school with such poor reading skills that they require what a spokesperson for the Council for Basic Education has called "dumbed down" textbooks in junior high and high school. During the past 15 years, public schools serving all types of communities have asked publishers for easier books in all academic subjects.

A history teacher in a suburban public high school cited as being one of the 79 best in the United States complained to me that when teachers were granted sabbaticals in his school they were urged to take courses in teaching reading, rather than in their subject areas. Reading problems are not confined to the inner city.

College students are also handicapped by inadequate reading skills. I began teaching undergraduate writing courses in a Big Ten university 20 years after I graduated from college. I was shocked to find that the textbooks for the course, designed for average freshmen and sophomores, was written at a level once considered appropriate for sixth grade. My students had difficulty reading samples of writing by authors which used to be considered standard fare for college undergraduates. A number also had problems understanding ordinary newspapers editorials. Instead of assigning this material as homework, I often found it necessary to lead students through these readings paragraph by paragraph. My students came from middle class homes and many had been educated in public schools considered to be better than average.

Are children in the United States less capable of learning to read than are European or Asian children? Are today's children less intelligent than students attending U.S. schools 30 or 40 years ago? Common sense and other evidence (including the need to revise the average score upward on a widely used intelligence test in 1972) tells us the answer to both questions is "no."

Why So Many Reading Problems?

Why, then, do two million *more* illiterate young adults emerge from our schools each year? Why are millions of children said to be "learning disabled" in reading, despite the lack of any scientifically valid test for identifying this mysterious malady? Why do average children from good homes need easier textbooks than their parents and grandparents used?

Educators often say that if children have difficulty learning to read it is because they come from homes where parents are illiterate or do not take the time to read to them. Educators have convinced many in the media and many citizens and legislators, as well, that uncaring parents and poor environment cause the illiteracy and other reading problems so prevalent in our nation's public schools. Yet I have heard complaints from scores of parents in all parts of the United States who

79

are themselves avid readers, parents who have diligently read to their child at home; still, their children have developed serious reading problems. Conversely, studies have shown that a number of inner city public schools in Houston, New York, and Philadelphia have achieved a success rate of 80 percent in teaching reading and other basic skills to poor and minority children, regardless of their home life and other out-of-school factors.

Given this evidence, we should not continue to accept the proposition that lack of ability on the part of American children, or poverty, or undesirable home life are to blame for this nation's shameful illiteracy. Instead, we should ask why some inner city public schools have a high rate of success in teaching poor, minority children to read, while in other public schools serving the same types of children, as many as 70 percent of the students are reading one or more years below grade level and 40 percent are reading two or more years below grade level.

Direct vs. Indirect Phonics

The primary difference between these two groups of schools is in the method used to teach reading. In the successful schools teachers use *direct phonics* (also called "code emphasis," "intensive phonics," "phonics first," or "synthetic phonics"). In the other schools, teachers use *indirect phonics* (also called "meaning emphasis," "eclectic," "psycholinguistic," or "analytic phonics").

It is important to understand the difference between these two methods of reading instruction. In direct teaching of phonics, children **learn at the very beginning—before they read stories—the sounds of** printed letters and letter combinations and how to pronounce words made up of these sounds. They learn these sounds systematically. For example: consonant sounds (p,t,k, etc.), short vowel sounds (*e* as in "wet," *a* as in "bat"), long vowel sounds (*i* as in "fire"), and so on. Once they begin reading stories, they are able to tackle new words by sound them out (decoding).

In indirect phonics, the teaching of sounds is not deliberate and systematic. Children are taught letter sounds only after they are taught to guess at the meanings of words by their shape or by their use in a sentence and to memorize lists of so-called "sight words." Instead of teaching all the letter sounds when children first begin learning to read, the indirect phonics method spreads the teaching of letter sounds over several years. Because indirect phonics requires so much word memorization and guessing, many children become frustrated, inadequate readers. At worst they leave school functionally illiterate—unable to use a phone book or read a medicine label. Other children have difficulty learning science or social studies because they cannot understand the textbooks. Still others taught by indirect phonics find reading such a disagreeable task that they avoid all reading not required for school work.

"Phony Phonics"

More than 100 research studies have shown that direct phonics is superior to indirect phonics with its heavy reliance on word guessing and memorization. Dr. Jeanne Chall of the Harvard University Graduate School of Education and author of *Learning to Read: The Great Debate*, updated edition (New York, McGraw-Hill, 1983) states that all children learn to read better if they are taught direct phonics.

Despite this overwhelming evidence in favor of the direct phonics method, it is used by only 15 percent of public schools in the United States. The other 85 percent use indirect phonics, the method proven to be less effective. Because indirect phonics stresses the look-say techniques of word memorization and guessing, rather than teaching children to sound out words, it is justly called "phony phonics." Unfortunately, the public is unaware of the vital difference between phony phonics and real (direct) phonics teaching. When parents, journalists, or legislators ask the people in charge of our public schools how they teach reading, they almost invariably answer, "We use phonics." In all but 15 percent of the cases, these school people are actually referring to phony phonics.

81

Children of all abilities in all types of communities throughout the United States are the losers in this confusion about reading methods. Inner city and minority children are usually the biggest losers when schools use the wrong teaching method. While middle class parents may be able to provide tutors for children who have reading problems, or may succeed in getting the school to provide special help, poor parents cannot afford tutors, and they may lack the self-assurance necessary to get special help from the school. Despite misteaching of reading, middle class children often learn to read well enough to get by, while poor children often do not.

Why Use Indirect Phonics?

If the vast majority of our children, regardless of background, are capable of learning to read, and if research has proved that direct phonics works best, why do only 15 percent of our public school primary teachers use this method of reading instruction? Our teachers do not use direct phonics in teaching children to read because they themselves have not been trained to use this method. Despite the research evidence that direct phonics is the best reading method, despite our growing illiteracy problem, our colleges of education continue to train prospective teachers and curriculum planners to use indirect phonics—teaching children to memorize and guess, with only a smattering of phonics.

We cannot blame teachers for poor reading instruction. Their college professors and the school district curriculum specialist tell them to use indirect phonics. The curriculum specialist also chooses the reading books. Not surprisingly, the books are based on the indirect phonics method. Like the general public, most teachers are not aware of the difference between this phony phonics and real phonics instruction. Many work very hard, unaware that they are using the wrong method. Occasionally they get fed up with the poor results of their efforts and look for a better method on their own. After they have had training in direct phonics, I have heard a number of these teachers exclaim, "Before I took this course, I thought I was really teaching phonics all along!" One teacher who switched to direct phonics after having used the other method for many years said: "We did nothing but sounds until December. Then we flew through the first few readers. I loved it! Every teacher (in other grades) in the school could spot the students who had been in those classes, they read so well."

Preventing Illiteracy

An overview of the research and my interviews with parents, teachers, and leading education specialists has convinced me that we have all the ingredients necessary to prevent illiteracy and the other reading problems which stand in the way of real reform in education:

1. Our spending for education is adequate.

2. The vast majority of our children in all types of communities are capable of learning to read in regular classrooms.

3. We have more than 100 research studies which point to direct phonics as the best method of teaching reading to all children.

4. Our primary teachers want to do a good job of teaching children to read. All they need is the correct method.

5. Parents care about their children's reading. When children have reading problems, parents who can afford it get help from private tutoring services. If parents were not concerned, tutoring would not be a growing business. Poor and minority parents try to get their children into those few inner city public schools which teach reading successfully. Some struggle to send their children to city parochial schools or to private schools operating on a shoestring, where teachers use the direct phonics reading method.

6. Children want to learn. Every one of those millions of adult illiterates was once a first-grader eager to learn to read. We should blame the teaching method—not the child or the adult who cannot read.

An Appeal for Direct Phonics

Why, when we have the necessary ingredients to teach children to read, do public schools still fail to do so, and instead add two million adult illiterates to our population each year? The evidence strongly suggests that the primary reason for illiteracy and our other serious reading problems is that our colleges of education promote ineffective classroom methods and fail to train prospective teachers to use direct phonics. Worse, education professors tell future teachers that if children are taught direct phonics they will be "word callers," unable to understand what they read. I heard this argument against direct phonics from nearly every primary teacher I interviewed. Yet the foremost researchers in reading all say that this argument is false. Dr. Chall quotes a study which states: "We have yet to encounter a student who could decode (sound out words) fluently but failed to comprehend." Decoding is what children learn to do with direct phonics.

While I do not suggest that this committee ignore the need to treat the symptoms of the reading problem by helping illiterate adults, I believe it should also give major attention to the prevention of illiteracy. It is far easier and less expensive to teach children to read correctly in the first place than it is to remedy the problem by teaching illiterate adults after they have experienced the frustration of trying to function without reading skills in our society.

READING NEEDS MORE THAN PHONICS

Dorothy Strickland

Dorothy Strickland, Ph.D., is a Professor of Education at Teachers College, Columbia University. She served as a member of the Commission on Reading that contributed to the report "Becoming a Nation of Readers." She also served as the past president of the International Reading Association.

Points to Consider:

1. What are cue systems and how do they work?
2. How does reading variety affect overall school achievement?
3. Why does the author encourage writing instruction in conjunction with reading?
4. What kind of instructional program does the author recommend?

Excerpted from testimony of Dorothy Strickland before the House Subcommittee on Elementary, Secondary, and Vocational Education of the House Committee on Education and Labor, March 20, 1986.

With a balanced approach we can help nurture students who can read material, understand it, and apply the meaning of what they have read. And that is the mark of an effective reader.

The teaching of reading has as its primary goal the production of literate individuals—individuals who can read in the fullest sense of the word. Reading competence signifies many things, including the ability to recognize and correctly pronounce words on a page, the ability to extract the appropriate meaning of words read and the ability to suitably use and apply the meaning of what is read. Reading is a many layered process whereby numerous interrelated elements of information are used by the reader to build meaning from written text. In short, reading is not a one-dimensional, simple process; it is a very complex one. The nature of the reading instruction we use in our schools must take this complexity into full account if we are to serve our students and our society well.

Effective reading ability is vital for a person to achieve his or her full potential in our complex society. Reading competence leads to individual independence and contributes immeasurably to the strength and vitality of our society.

Cue Systems

In considering the question of reading and reading instruction, several important points must be made.

The first is that reading and literacy learning are constructive processes. That is, the learner's knowledge of language and of the world is a vital foundation for reading ability. As the reader reads, he or she makes use of a variety of cues or cue systems. These important cue systems include letter/sound relationships (phonics), word meanings, and language structure. For effective reading to occur, all of these cue systems must operate.

A simple example will illustrate the function of these three elements and demonstrate that they are inextricably and inevitably related. Consider the simple word *mean*. This word consists of four different letters and occurs quite frequently in our daily language. Next, consider the following sentences in which the word *mean* is used:

Hansel and Gretel had a mean stepmother.
This trip will mean a lot to him.
I didn't mean it!
The mean was not appropriate to the end.
I didn't mean strawberry, I meant cherry.

Here we see a clear example of how three cue systems must operate in order for successful reading to occur. Certainly letter and sound relationships are important to the successful pronunciation of the word *mean.* But pronunciation is not, of itself, sufficient for correct reading to occur in all of the examples seen here. Word meaning in different contexts must be discerned through a process of using knowledge of language structure, alternative word meanings, and the reader's experience to confirm the appropriate denotation of the word. In other words, three important cue systems or strategies must be used if successful reading is to occur.

Reading instruction which makes full use of these important cue systems is the most effective instruction for the beginning reader. To provide the student with a constrained repertoire of reading strategies, such as one limited to mere decoding or sounding-out, is to promote a very narrow, limited reading capability. One would not argue that the ability to decode, by itself, constitutes the ability to read. If that were the case then the person who mastered, for example, the French alphabet could claim to be able to "read" French, even though a total lack of comprehension might exist. Is this realistic or desirable? Understanding the message should be the ultimate goal of reading and, therefore, must be an integral part of reading instruction from the very beginning.

Reading Variety

Skilled readers are also wide readers. That is, the skill of reading should lead to the habit of reading widely on a variety of subjects. According to the report, *What Works,* recently released by the U.S. Department of Education, reading fluency and vocabulary are increased through extensive independent reading. Such reading, especially when it is organized around the reading of good literature, builds background knowledge while exposing the child to a rich variety of language and meaning. All of these elements clearly contribute to better reading ability.

There is a well-documented and pervasive relationship between overall school achievement and reading. Students who read a lot not only read better, but they also do better in most other aspects of school as well. Students who read well also read voluntarily and often; they seek information, experience, and personal growth through reading. Research shows that meaningful context enhances the word identification and comprehension process and that reading is not merely a serial process of letter-by-letter decoding. The fact that wide and frequent reading improves overall reading achievement is an important piece of evidence in this regard.

Writing is Important

The strong relationship between reading and writing demonstrates the importance of a broad, constructive approach to reading instruction. A considerable body of sound research clearly demonstrates that writing is a powerful promoter of reading competence. Good writers are also good readers, and good reading programs should offer many opportunities for student writing. Studies of young children have shown that writing helps them to develop their language abilities and that these language abilities, in turn, promote better reading. Reading and writing instruction should start early and lead to life-long competencies and habits. These competencies and habits are desirable because they expand possibilities and remove limitations and, by so doing, they enable a fuller achievement of human potential. In short, limited and narrowly defined reading instruction can lead to limited abilities on the part of the reader.

Children "at Risk"

There is a disparity between achievers and non-achievers in our society. The recent report on reading achievement by the National Assessment of Educational Progress makes this point quite clearly. Students who are drawn from segments of society that are often outside the mainstream of our nation's economic life display levels of reading achievement that are significantly below those of other groups. These students are making impressive gains but a gap in achievement still exists.

A large number of such students are enrolled in Chapter I programs. These students need our help. Why limit them? They need instructional programs that give them all the reading strategies they require to be better, more capable readers. For these students, simple decoding is not enough. They must have the benefits of learning how to use all of the necessary reading cue systems: letter/sound relationships, word meanings, and language structure. They need to be encouraged to read widely and taught how to use the information they can gain through reading. If we allow these children who are "at risk" to be deprived of extra help, the gap between the "haves" and the "have nots" will widen.

We Need Balanced Programs

We have learned a great deal about how people learn to read and what that means for classroom instruction. The research that has been carried out and reported through the many programs of study encouraged by the federal government has borne fruit. We know that reading is a constructive and complex process involving many elements. Phonics is only one of the strategies used to make sense of print. One cannot deny the function of letter/sound knowledge in beginning reading; nor can one reasonably oppose the careful, intelligent, and balanced teaching of phonics in early reading instruction.

Whether or not phonics is effective is not the issue here. The issue is the negative and limiting effect of an overly-simplified concept of what constitutes reading and effective reading programs. Don't limit our students' potential by limiting reading instruction to a single, rigidly defined approach. Our students, our developing readers, must have all the benefits of our present knowledge of the reading and learning process. We must encourage the development of the richest programs of instruction possible at the earliest age to be certain that students receive all they can from our efforts. No one wishes to promote or protect ineffective reading instruction. We must apply what we know to be true about the reading and learning process if we are to be successful and do the best we can for the school children of America.

I ask you to remember that reading is more than a simple, easily defined set of skills. It is a complex process involving many elements— elements which good instructional programs incorporate in a wide variety of ways. With a balanced approach we can help nurture students who can read material, understand it, and apply the meaning of what they have read. And that is the mark of an effective reader.

PRIVATE INDUSTRY MUST LEAD THE FIGHT AGAINST ILLITERACY

Northeast-Midwest Institute

The Northeast-Midwest Institute is a private, nonprofit organization devoted to research and public education on issues of regional concern. Since the Institute was established in 1977, its primary goal has been to insure that federal policies are geographically equitable and responsive to the needs of the 18-state region that long has formed the nation's industrial heartland. The Institute's primary constituency is policy makers from the Northeast and Midwest.

Points to Consider:

1. How many companies identified writing deficiencies among their employees?
2. What percentage of company training funds are spent on remedial education?
3. Why is the Ford-United Auto Workers approach a model for remedial education programs?
4. How can companies get involved in community-based adult literacy efforts?

Excerpted from testimony of the Northeast-Midwest Institute before the House Subcommittee on Elementary, Secondary, and Vocational Education of the House Committee on Education and Labor, August 1, 1985.

Businesses must mobilize their resources to increase employee literacy in ways that are consistent with their own needs for productivity in increasingly competitive world markets.

Employers recognize that the lack of basic skills among Americans is of crisis proportions in many parts of the employment market. And the problem can only worsen, if, as some economists predict, the United States faces impending labor shortages in the coming decade. Businesses must mobilize their resources to increase employee literacy in ways that are consistent with their own needs for productivity in increasingly competitive world markets.

The Center for Public Resources, a private, nonprofit organization, surveyed employers nationally in 1982 to determine the extent of basic skill deficiencies among their employees.

- More than one-half the responding companies identified writing deficiencies among their secretarial, skilled labor, managerial, supervisory, and bookkeeping personnel. The most frequently cited problems were poor grammar, spelling, and punctuation.
- Over one-half found inadequacies in mathematics in a wide range of employees, from semi-skilled laborers to bookkeepers.
- More than one-half identified deficiencies in speaking and listening skills among secretarial, clerical, service, supervisory, and managerial personnel.
- Over two-thirds noted that basic skills deficiencies limit the company's ability to promote employees, both high school graduates and nongraduates.

The study concluded:

> While school respondees often cited vocational skills as the most important factor in youth employability, the business view was that if schools provided adequately educated youth, business would provide, indeed overwhelmingly does provide, technical training. What business decidedly indicated it did not want to do, but is in fact doing, is to educate its employees in ninth- and tenth-grade skills.[1]

Companies can provide programs to upgrade their employees' basic skills.... Although examples can be found, company-sponsored in-house programs focused solely on remediation account for only a small fraction of private-sector training investments. One recent study found that only 8 percent of courses offered by employers during working hours are basic remedial courses. The American Society for Training and Development, an association of private-sector human resources managers, estimates that less than 1 percent of company training funds are spent on remedial education. Even so, corporate participants in a recent series of forums on business and education felt

90

SIGNIFICANT COSTS

Illiteracy costs the USA about $225 billion annually in lost industrial productivity, unrealized tax revenues, welfare and unemployment payments, and the cost of crime and prisons.

USA Today, *September 10, 1987*

that business is spending too much time and money on remedial training in communications and other basic skills. Typical company programs are geared to new entry-level employees and are combined with training in the company's operations. Often they are partially supported by federal job training funds aimed at the disadvantaged. Only very large corporations with major in-house training capacities are likely to find it efficient to cover the entire cost of their own basic literacy training . . . .

Company policy also calls for the definition and measurement of program objectives beforehand. Standards should be set for measuring success in terms of participants' job behavior, not merely their ability to pass tests. Any program should have realistic goals tied to practical business needs—the development and maintainence of a proficient and motivated work force. The program also should be evaluated systematically.

As this policy suggests, **companies may do well to contract with educational institutions or community-based organizations for their employees' remedial needs** . . . .This approach can be used by companies planning to shut down or relocate. . . .

Perhaps the best-known dislocated workers programs are the ongoing efforts sponsored by the United Auto Workers (UAW) in cooperation with Ford and General Motors. The UAW-Ford model emphasizes the necessity of combining community resources to help the newly unemployed. In the Milpitas plant closing in San Jose, for example, Ford and the UAW contracted with the local adult education office to provide courses at the plant, including remedial math and reading. Eight hundred persons altogether participated in adult education, and 183 received high school diplomas or GEDs. The UAW-Ford program recognizes remedial education as an important, sometimes crucial, component in an overall worker-readjustment strategy. It is this new mastery of the basics that increases workers' self-confidence and opportunities for reemployment. Other dislocated worker programs have duplicated the UAW-Ford approach . . . .

In addition to working on specific literacy needs of their own employees, both current and former, companies contribute to the solution of the national illiteracy crisis by forming partnerships with educational institutions and community-based groups to improve basic skills. . . .

Companies also must become more broadly involved in policy-making, resource allocation, and planning for their local secondary school systems as a whole. Business leaders are joining top-echelon educational administrators and contributing their resources, time, and expertise to designing system improvements. Many of these efforts focus on basic skills. The goal is to improve the quality of literacy training in the community's secondary school system so as to raise the average skill levels of new entrants into the work force. . . .

Many industry-education collaborations were spurred by the well-publicized critiques of the nation's school systems, especially *A Nation at Risk,* the report of the National Commission on Excellence in Education in 1983. However, the Commission on Higher Education and the Adult Learner pointed out that the excellence commission limited its recommendations to reforms in the education of youth, reinforcing the idea that learning is only for the young and that adults have completed their schooling. . . .

Companies can target their concern and activities on adult illiterates in the wider community beyond the schools. Businesses should involve themselves in community-based adult literacy efforts and programs in adult basic education. Company actions are wide ranging. Numerous corporations are contributing funds to public literacy awareness efforts at national, state, and local levels. The Ashland Oil Corporation provided a major grant through its charitable foundation to the Kentucky educational television network for a campaign encouraging adults to earn their GED certificates. . . . IBM Corporation makes grants to community-based organizations as part of its commitment to the literacy movement. . . .

Companies can encourage their employees to participate in community-based volunteer programs. B. Dalton Bookseller, already involved in many adult education strategies in the 500 communities where its outlets are located, recently undertook a campaign to enlist employees on all levels to tutor adults in basic skills. . . .

Some companies have opened their in-house remedial programs to the larger community. In Winston-Salem, North Carolina, R.J. Reynolds Tobacco Company uses the services of Forsyth Technical Institute to provide an in-plant adult basic education program. The program is open to dislocated workers in the community as well. . . .

Companies can use their political power and connections to influence decisions on funds and priorities for public institutions. Business groups already have formed in Memphis, New Orleans, and Cincinnati to work for the passage of tax levies to benefit education. Efforts of individual companies to ease the literacy crisis are important, but in the long run, success will depend on collective efforts to influence policy in state capitals and in Washington. Companies must organize themselves into highly focused coalitions to provide sustained support to the public institutions whose job it is to equip people with the basic skills required by the labor market.

Some employers already have decried basic skills deficiencies in their workers and in job applicants. Others are concerned that employees facing termination lack the elementary skills to find new jobs or take advantage of retraining. At the present time, most companies have ample choices in a slack labor market. Yet in the next decade demographic change—an aging work force and a pool of younger applicants increasingly comprised of the educationally and economically disadvantaged—could reduce the range of choice. "Literacy for all" is becoming as much an economic imperative as it is a social and cultural one.

¹James F. Henry, "Expectations of the Workplace: Basic Skills in the U.S. Workforce," in *Functional Literacy and the Workplace* (Washington, D.C.: American Council of Life Insurance, 1984), p. 23.

14 DEALING WITH ILLITERACY

THE FEDERAL GOVERNMENT MUST LEAD THE WAY

Richard C. Anderson

Richard C. Anderson is the director of the Center for the Study of Reading at the University of Illinois. This center is sponsored by the National Institute of Education.

Points to Consider:

1. According to the author, why does reading seldom receive attention in federal decisionmaking?
2. How much money does the author want the National Institute of Education to spend on reading research?
3. What elements are involved in quality education?
4. If resources are scarce, is it better to fund early education or later years in schooling? Why?

Excerpted from testimony of Richard C. Anderson before the House Subcommittee on Elementary, Secondary, and Vocational Education of the House Committee on Education and Labor, October 1, 1985.

In education it appears to be doubly true that an ounce of prevention is worth a pound of cure. There is no substitute for quality early education that gets all, or most, children off to a good start in learning to read.

I urge you to read the report, *Becoming a Nation of Readers*. As chairman of the commission that produced the report, and one of its principal authors, I am proud to say that it has been widely acclaimed as the most authoritative statement available on literacy.

I am going to make three points. They are rather simple points, might even be thought to be obvious, but I think they do provide a foundation for federal policy in the area of literacy. . . .

Make Reading the Highest Federal Education Priority

Reading is the cornerstone of excellence in education and beyond. Reading is basic to all other achievement, whether in the sciences, in business, in government, or in the arts. Taking the perspective of the society, a nation of non-readers is not fit to choose its own leaders or make its own laws, and it will not long continue to compete successfully with other societies during the Information Age. Taking the perspective of the individual, a child who is a non-reader is a family tragedy; it is not an exaggeration to say that a failure to learn to read is the educational equivalent of cancer.

But I know that you already know that there are good and sufficient reasons why reading is the first of the three *R*s. Why, then, do I remind you of the centrality of reading?

The answer is that over a period of many years my experience has been that reading seldom gets weighted in proportion to its importance in federal decisionmaking. One of the reasons for this fact is the way that government decisionmaking works: Every little special interest group gets something; every issue, big or small, receives at least some attention. I do not suppose that education is any more divided than other fields, so I do not intend this as a special criticism of the federal education establishment, past or present. Still, because of a false even-handedness, when the pie is sliced, reading gets a smaller piece than it ought to have considering its importance.

As a citizen, I do not expect members of Congress to be experts on such matters as whether the short *a* sound should be taught before the long *a* sound, but I believe I should be able to expect the Congress to use its powers of budgeting, authorization, appropriation, and oversight to assure that reading gets attention commensurate with its importance as a national priority.

Specifically, as a reading researcher, I believe that the Congress should encourage the National Institute of Education to spend $4-5 million a year, or approximately 8-10 percent of its present annual budget, directly on reading research (in addition to monies spent on such topics as writing and effective elementary schools that may contribute indirectly to knowledge about reading). About half of this money should fund a strong national center for reading research, the remainder a program of smaller, shorter-term projects.

Beware of Simplistic Solutions

I have already compared a failure to learn to read with cancer. Like cancer, reading failure provokes strong reactions. People have passionate convictions about the cause of reading failure and its cure. Sometimes these beliefs are clearly wrong; usually, at best, the beliefs represent an incomplete understanding of reading and reading instruction.

As we wrote in *Becoming a Nation of Readers,* "Based on what we now know, it is incorrect to suppose that there is a simple or single step which, if taken correctly, will immediately allow a child to read. Becoming a skilled reader is a journey that involves many steps. Similarly, it is unrealistic to anticipate that some one critical feature of instruction will be discovered which, if in place, will assure rapid progress in reading. Quality instruction involves many elements. Strengthening any one element yields small gains. For large gains, many elements must be in place." We need good teachers who are well trained. We need

Becoming a Nation of Readers:

Implications for Teachers

Office of Educational
Research and Improvement
U.S. Department of Education
Programs for the
Improvement of Practice

According to its authors, *Becoming a Nation of Readers* is the first major report directly applicable to improving classroom reading instruction.

much better books for our children than the publishing industry is now providing. We need more access to library books, both fiction and non-fiction, particularly for poor children. We need teachers who teach using content and method based on the best knowledge now available. This happens in our best classrooms, but in many classrooms it does not.

We need schools with an ethos that supports literacy, where literacy gets as high a priority as the performance of the athletic teams and the performances of the band, the orchestra, and the chorus. We need order and discipline, collegiality. We need opportunities for advancing knowledge and continued renewal on the part of teachers. . . .

Invest in Early Childhood and Primary School Education

It is surely wise social policy to work toward reforming high schools, improving colleges, and eliminating adult illiteracy. However, if resources are scarce and hard choices must be made, research strongly suggests that there is a better yield from investments in early education, when children are beginning to learn to read. Economics research on human capital formation establishes that a society receives a greater return on investment in elementary education than investment in later years of schooling. Long-term educational research shows that quality early education for children at risk for educational failure produces an array of lasting benefits including increased test scores, increased rates of high school graduation and college attendance, and reduced rates of special education referral, delinquency, crime, teenage pregnancy, and dependence on welfare. Moreover, the research suggests that early education is more effective and less costly than programs to cure problems once they have arisen.

Thus, in education it appears to be doubly true that an ounce of prevention is worth a pound of cure. There is no substitute for quality early education that gets all, or most, children off to a good start in learning to read.

EXAMINING COUNTERPOINTS

This activity may be used an an individualized study guide for students in libraries and resource centers or as a discussion catalyst in small group and classroom discussions.

The Point

The federal government should increase funding to our nation's schools. More money is needed to strengthen the programs of our elementary and secondary school system. Quality education, backed by federal support, is the most important intervention in reducing the levels of illiteracy found in today's population.

The Counterpoint

The federal government should not increase funding to our nation's schools. In 1983, federal expenditures totaled $230 million—more than double what the government spent on education 10 years earlier. Despite this increased spending, the illiteracy rate continues to rise. Money alone is not the answer.

Guidelines

Part A

Examine the counterpoints above and then consider the following questions.

1. Do you agree more with the point or counterpoint? Why?

2. Which reading in this book best illustrates the point?

3. Which reading best illustrates the counterpoint?

4. Do any cartoons in this book illustrate the meaning of the point or counterpoint arguments? Which ones and why?

Part B

Social issues are usually complex, but often problems become over-simplified in political debates and discussions. Usually a polarized version of social conflict does not adequately represent the diversity of views that surround social conflicts. Examine the counterpoints. Then write down other possible interpretations of this issue than the two arguments stated in the counterpoints.

CHAPTER 3

THE SOCIAL FOUNDATIONS OF EDUCATIONAL FAILURE

15 THE SOCIAL FOUNDATIONS OF EDUCATIONAL FAILURE

MINORITY CHILDREN AT RISK

Samuel L. Banks

Dr. Samuel L. Banks is the national president of the Association for the Study of Afro-American Life and History, Inc. and the supervisor of Social Studies for the Baltimore City Public Schools.

Points to Consider:

1. According to the author, why does illiteracy exist in the United States?
2. How many students drop out of school each year?
3. What does the author mean by "custodial education"?
4. How has the Reagan Administration hindered educational opportunity for minority children?

Excerpted from testimony of Samuel L. Banks before the House Subcommittee on Elementary, Secondary, and Vocational Education of the House Committee on Education and Labor, October 1, 1985.

A child's social class, race, ethnicity, where he or she lives, or point of national origin must not be the primary determinant as to whether he or she receives the highest quality of education our nation can afford.

I am profoundly honored to address the urgent and proliferating problems of illiteracy and urgent steps necessary to ameliorate "basic skills of black students." You and your colleagues have rendered a major contribution to our nation in holding these hearings in order to provide succor and educational uplift for the educationally excluded, dispossessed, and alienated in our nation.

A National Disgrace

As you and the members of these subcommittees are fully aware, the existence of over 24 million functional illiterates in our nation, disproportionately black and Hispanics, constitutes a national disgrace. This lamentable and appalling condition exists in the most prosperous nation in the world because we have not made a demonstrable commitment to end this scourge (i.e., illiteracy) of our nation. There is, to be sure, a painful socio-racial nexus between poverty and educational attainment. Most functional illiterates in our nation are white, but black and Hispanics represent the largest percentage of the poor and functional illiterates.

This morning, I speak in the capacity of national president of the Association for the Study of Afro-American Life and History, Inc. The Association for the Study of Afro-American Life and History, Inc. (ASALH), founded by the late Dr. Carter Godwin Woodson on September 9, 1915 in Chicago, is a national organization of black historians, educators, academicians, and lay people committed to serious research, study, and dissemination of information on black life and culture. Dr. Woodson's seminal work, *The Mis-Education of the Negro,* published over 50 years ago, represents a potent and enduring work focusing on the critical needs of black children and what is needed for enhancement and substantive improvement.

As one reviews the 16,000 school districts in our nation serving over 41 million students, especially urban children and youths, the disquieting reality of the mis-education, under-education, and non-education of black and poor children continues in a nation with a gross national product in excess of $2 trillion. This situation prevails in spite of the valiant, sacrificial, and heroic efforts of educators in large urban school districts such as Boston; New York; Philadelphia; Baltimore; Chicago; St. Louis; Richmond, Virginia; Los Angeles, and other urban school districts. The linchpin necessary for demonstrable excellence and equal educational opportunity boils down to a national commitment and requisite human and monetary resources. Until a sustained and concentrated national commitment is made to close the historic socio-racial and fiscal chasm between urban and suburban school districts, separate and unequal education will continue in our nation. The socioeconomic pathologies which flow from this lamentable situation—as reflected in school dropouts (now approaching 2 million a year), crime, and other deviant behavior—will accelerate and expand. The end result will be a further fiscal and human drain on the body politic.

It, too, is significant to observe, beginning with the *Nation at Risk* report warning the nation of a "rising tide of mediocrity" and 11 other major reports, that black Americans except in a tertiary or peripheral manner were largely ignored or relegated to the national back burner. If it had not been for the reports of the National Alliance of Black Educators and the Association for the Study of Afro-American Life and History (ASALH), the doleful and shoddy state of the preponderant number of over 9 million black children and youths would have been consigned to further indifference and neglect.

Specific Recommendations

I am heartened and encouraged that when I appointed ASALH's national task force on "Excellence in Education: A Black Perspective," in Washington, D.C., in October 1984 chaired by Dr. Herman Brown, distinguished Professor of Psychology at the University of the District

of Columbia, the educational needs of black children and youths were given recognition. Dr. Brown was joined by Mrs. Elizabeth Edmonds, principal of Northern Senior High School, Baltimore, Md.; Dr. Gwendolyn Cooke, principal of the Lemmel Middle School, Baltimore, Md.; Dr. June L. Harris, legislative analyst, House Education and Labor Committee; Dr. Samuel L. Banks, national president of ASALH and supervisor of Social Studies, Baltimore City Public Schools. Each of these highly respected educators, on their own time and without pay, rendered distinctive and selfless service. Our report, *Excellence in Education: A Black Perspective,* contains 72 recommendations and 15 basic conclusions in terms of what we deem is critical for the resuscitation and revitalization of urban education. A central thread that pervades our report is that equality of educational opportunity should be made available now to all of our children and youths.

I am providing the following specific recommendations, as matters of urgency for the consideration of the subcommittees:

1. Full and equal financial support by federal, state, and local governments.

2. Full and vigorous enforcement of the *Brown* decisions of 1954-1955 and subsequent federal court decisions in support of equal educational opportunities.

3. Concentrated emphasis on multiethnic and multicultural education, in all subject areas, that accentuate positive self-concept and analytical thinking. Multiethnic education should be mandated by school board policy.

4. Requirements that all textbooks, especially in science, English, history and social science classes, and fine arts classes (i.e., art and music) be multiethnic.

5. Requirement that textbook publishers utilize black and minority writers in the conceptualization and writing of textbooks and instructional materials. School boards should establish this as a matter of policy.

6. Insistence on high quality education at all levels (i.e., elementary, secondary, higher education). The concept of custodial education or simply keeping children and youths from downtown or off the street must be ended now.

7. Work in concert with black churches, civic groups, sororities, fraternities, and social groups to reestablish a sense of community and caring.

8. Assiduous efforts to support and maintain high quality, predominantly black institutions of higher education.

9. Careful review and appropriate action to curb the disproportionate placement of black students in special education classes or non-college preparatory classes.

10. Development of challenging and appropriate vocational and technical programs related to current and future job demands. Conversely, dead-end and inadequate vocational programs should be eliminated.

11. Development of strategies to maximize and sustain black students in academic and gifted programs. Black students are seriously under represented in advanced academic, gifted, and technical programs.

12. Development of strategies and techniques to curb the disproportionate level of black suspensions, expulsions, and dropouts.

13. Increase the number of assignments requiring writing, speaking, problem solving, and critical thinking, as well as oral exercises.

14. Placement and grouping of students, as well as promotion and graduation policies, should be guided by the academic progress of students and their learning and instructional needs, rather than by age and the concept of social promotion.

15. To assess school board membership needs in terms of background, skills, and diversity (ethnic, racial, sexual, age, geographic, social, and political). The school board should reflect the population of the school district.

16. Title I must be funded at full authorization and expanded.

17. Predominantly black schools should be considered as effective schools with all the necessary finance, budget, books, and administrative support provided white schools.

18. Techniques of desegregating schools (pupil assignment, faculty and staff assignment, pupil transportation, site selection, construction policies, etc.) (redrawing zone lines, pairing and grouping schools, modified feeder patterns, skip zoning, optional zones, open enrollment, transfers, magnet schools, special programs, metropolitan cooperation,

open housing, etc.) should not put the burden of proof on black schools. (Costs, neighborhood school mystique, busing, etc.)

19. That public schools should develop techniques to build up positive self-concepts in black children, as well as eliminate the concept of a deficient deficit model.

20. Teachers' starting salaries should be equivalent to starting salaries for college graduates in the corporate world.

21. That all teachers in the elementary schools and junior high schools be subject matter specialists beginning with the third grade level. Subject matter specialists should be in the fields of reading, social studies, science, mathematics, literature, writing, and the areas of critical thinking and oral discourse (i.e., communication). Elementary teachers cannot be specialists in all subjects (reading, writing, language arts, arithmetic, science, social sciences, etc.), so subject matter specialists should be hired.

22. Student incentives to remain in school should include: work/study programs, academic credit for experiential learning, financial assistance, cooperative education, internships, and apprenticeships.

23. Development of a career ladder program (i.e., Apprentice, Tenured, Master) for all teachers as a means of incentive and enhancing morale.

24. Provision for full-time librarians and counselors in elementary and secondary schools.

25. Closer articulation between vocational education and the world of work. Instruction should be geared to practical realities and demands of industry.

Cutbacks Are Not Helping

In conclusion, it must be noted that President Reagan's espousal of supply-side economics and the "New Federalism" has exacerbated the tenuous and marginal socioeconomic status of black Americans and the poor. The drastic cutbacks in federal support for education, nutritional programs, housing, day care, health care, and other vital social programs have placed an additional onus or strain on the nations's urban schools and society at large. Unemployment among black youths in urban centers is approximately 53 percent and the rate of unemployment for black adults is 14 percent. The total level of unemployment for all Americans for July 1982, according to the Bureau of Labor Statistics, was 10.5 million. The figure is now approximately 8 million.

Nonetheless, keeping faith with their forebearers, black Americans must set their hands to the plow and work assiduously and unremittingly, as in the past, for top-quality education. It remains the passport to survival, upward mobility, and success in the United States.

Today, a mood of retreat, obfuscation, and hostility to human and civil rights, *Brown* included, engulfs our nation. A national presidential administration, led by President Ronald Wilson Reagan, exhorts the nation to support tuition vouchers, tax credits for private schools, a frontal assault on the principle of affirmative action, and an end to busing as one of many tools to achieve school desegregation. In point of fact, the Reagan Administration has urged over 50 communities across the nation to forswear affirmative action programs, and to be assured of the support of the federal government in obstructing the implementation of active affirmative action programs.

Bleak Situation

The situation is equally bleak for over 9 million black children and youths in the nation's public schools. The federal government, in the celebrated Norfolk, Virginia school case which seeks to resegregate black students, has joined the case on the side of the Norfolk School Board as amicus curiae. The Norfolk City Public School System, as was true of the well-known Prince Edward County, Virginia Public Schools, closed its doors in 1959 rather than desegregate in compliance with the *Brown* decisions. We now have the painful irony of the national government seeking to help a recalcitrant Norfolk City School Board in its efforts to resegregate black children. Additionally, the Reagan Administration pledges support to other school districts (viz., Little Rock, Prince George's, Maryland, etc.) which seek to resegregate black children.

Black parents must remain constant, steadfast, and vigilant in supporting hard-earned educational rights and opportunities provided by the *Brown* decisions and subsequent federal court decisions. An operational pragmatism constitutes a centrality for black Americans supporting equality of educational opportunity. Operational pragmatism posits the belief that where the children of the white culture are enrolled, the educational resources, human and monetary, necessary for demonstrable educational excellence will be provided.

Equal educational opportunity represents the basis for the empowerment of black Americans and socioeconomic mobility in the American social order. Black Americans and fair-minded citizens must not permit a deferral of this long overdue process.

In summary, racial bifurcation or duality continues in American education at all levels (i.e., elementary-secondary and higher education). The overwhelming number of the 9 million black children in elementary and secondary schools and 1 million in institutions of higher education are the recipients of separate and unequal education notwithstanding the momentous *Brown* decisions of 1954 and 1955 and subsequent federal court decisions. In short, equity and excellence in education are far distant and elusive realities for black and poor students in our nation. Our nation, to date, has failed to mobilize the commitment and resources, human and monetary, to ensure equality of educational opportunity and excellence for all children and youths. Now is the time to begin in earnest.

Hapless Victims

Even as we sit and interact in this salubrious and majestic setting on historic and awe-inspiring Capitol Hill, we are on the verge of losing another generation of black and impoverished youngsters in urban school districts, predominantly black, Hispanic, and poor, throughout our nation. These youngsters, essentially, are the hapless victims of inadequate human and monetary resources and monumental national indifference. It is in the national interest that the federal government seize the initiative in urban areas, as was done so nobly and creatively for war-devastated Europe in "turning the lights on again" through the massive and sustained Marshall Plan which cost in excess of 15 billion dollars between 1945-1948.

The time, I believe, is long overdue to turn the educational, political, and economic lights on in the sprawling urban centers of our nation. Horace Mann, a seminal and indefatigable advocate of public education, saw public education as the "equalizer of the conditions of men (women)." We should now, through a sustained, assiduous, and genuine national effort, redeem Mann's earnest belief for all of our citizens.

John Gardner offers a highly potent and urgent admoninition in his thoughtful book, *Excellence,* for all of us. "A nation is never finished. You can't build it and then leave it standing as the Pharaohs did the pyramids. It has to be recreated for each generation by believing, caring men and women. It is now our turn. If we don't care, nothing can save the nation. If we believe and care, nothing can stop us."

I repeat a constant of my testimony: We have to truly care and act in support of equity and equality of opportunity for all Americans. A child's social class, race, ethnicity, where he or she lives, or point of national origin must not be the primary determinant as to whether he or she receives the highest quality of education our nation can afford. It is, decidedly, in our national interest to move forward affirmatively, fairly, and speedily.

16 THE SOCIAL FOUNDATIONS OF EDUCATIONAL FAILURE

GREAT PROGRESS IN EDUCATIONAL REFORM

David P. Gardner

David P. Gardner is the president of the University of California. He was also the chairman of the National Commission on Excellence in Education, created by Secretary of Education T. H. Bell under the Reagan Administration. The Commission published a report on the quality of education in America called A Nation at Risk: The Imperative for Educational Reform.

Points to Consider:

1. How do teacher salaries compare to professionals with similar training and experience?
2. Why is the idea of a learning society considered practical?
3. What functions could the federal government provide in the task of educational reform?
4. What was the central message of *A Nation at Risk*?

Excerpted from testimony of David P. Gardner before the House Sub-committee on Elementary, Secondary, and Vocational Education of the House Committee on Education and Labor, October 1, 1985.

The educational reform movement has achieved remarkable gains in a remarkably short time.

My purpose this morning is to put the matter of illiteracy within the broader context of educational reform in the United States. Since the publication in 1983 of the National Commission on Excellence in Education's report, *A Nation at Risk,* more than a dozen national reports have called for far-reaching reform in our educational system. The nation's response to this call for reform has been clear, direct, and overwhelmingly on the side of major changes to improve schooling in America.

Educational Reform

In fact, the first thing to be said about the educational reform movement is that it has achieved remarkable gains in a remarkably short time. Much of the reason, it seems to me, is that change occurred where it counts most: in states, localities, districts, and individual schools.

But the second thing to be said about the educational reform movement is that it is far from over. We are now in the process of coupling with more effect than in the past our educational aims, policies, programs, and practice. So, this is an excellent vantage point from which to look at aspects of educational reform that need more attention.

Important Issues

I believe there are several important issues that need to be addressed. All were included in *A Nation at Risk* but have received less attention than they might have or demand more attention than they seem to be getting.

First, *A Nation at Risk* called for improvements in the recruitment, training, and working conditions of teachers by recommending that teacher salaries be increased generally and that salaries be professionally competitive, market sensitive, and performance based. Many states and localities have tried hard to do so. But the gap between what teachers can expect to make and what other professionals with similar training and experience can earn is still unacceptably high.

Improvement is all the more important in light of predicted teacher shortages in some states and in some disciplines nationwide. At the same time, the need to recruit more teachers presents us with the opportunity to experiment with alternative routes to the teaching profession, an opportunity we should embrace. As a separate but related matter, we need to work harder on finding ways to evaluate teacher performance that are sufficiently sensitive and demonstrably objective.

Second, *A Nation at Risk* recognized that a rigorous program in the fine and performing arts ought to be a part of the education of our high school students. Moreover, we must dispense with the idea that these

111

A Nation At Risk:

THE IMPERATIVE FOR EDUCATIONAL REFORM

A Report to the Nation
and the
Secretary of Education
United States Department of Education
by
The National Commission on Excellence in Education

April 1983

The National Commission on Excellence in Education, created by Secretary of Education T.H. Bell, produced *A Nation at Risk,* a report that defines and offers solutions to the problems in American education.

disciplines are somehow less serious in intent and execution than other kinds of courses. They are not frills and should not be regarded as such. We should give as much attention to the quality of instruction in the programs in the arts as we give to the quality in science and mathematics and English. This valuable dimension of the high school curriculum needs more attention, support, and encouragement.

Third, critics of *A Nation at Risk* have argued that our insistence upon rigorous standards and high expectations for students means that we run the risk of losing students to early failure and discouragement. We, of course, already are losing students to early failure and discouragement. But, on the contrary, raising standards means that we have to pay more attention than ever to the diversity of students in our classrooms.

Some states and localities have made strenuous efforts to pay attention to the differences among students while at the same time requiring high standards of performance, but more work needs to be done in this area. We need more information and more research on how students learn. Only by understanding that complex process can we give them the tools to take responsibility for learning throughout their lives.

Fourth, *A Nation at Risk* insisted on the fact that learning, despite its public aspects and its central importance to the public good, is essentially a private activity and demands student effort. Parents, teachers, school board members, legislators, and governors can help. Only students can make learning happen. William Raspberry, a nationally syndicated columnist, put it succinctly in a recent column: "Learning," he said, "is not a passive exercise. It is not something that happens to you if you can get yourself into the right place. It is work. It may be relatively pleasant work for those lucky enough to love learning, but it is still work."

In the last pages of *A Nation at Risk,* we address a short note to parents; and we address a short note to students in which we set forth what we think are their respective obligations and responsibilities to improve the schools and learning in them.

It may be a truism, but it is surely relevant to education and all too often overlooked. We must increase the ways by which we recognize student academic achievement, just as we recognize student athletic achievement. *A Nation at Risk,* in fact, set as an overall goal of educational reform the creation of a learning society, defined as a commitment for all to seek and for education to offer, the opportunity to stretch their minds to full capacity through life-long learning.

The idea of a learning society is not simply idealistic. It is eminently practical. The nation needs skilled and educated people not only to meet the needs of our technological economy but also to make our complex democracy work through the creation of an informed citizenry.

Fifth, *A Nation at Risk* sought to define the appropriate role of the federal government in the task of educational reform. We recognize that

113

our decentralized system of education meant that the principal responsibility for action lay with the states and local jurisdictions. But we believed there were functions the federal government in cooperation with states and localities is especially equipped to fulfill: meeting the needs of key groups of students such as the gifted and talented, the socioeconomically disadvantaged, and minority and language-minority students, protecting constitutional and civil rights for students and school personnel, collecting data about education generally, supporting curriculum improvement and research and teaching, learning, and the management of schools, supporting teacher training in areas of critical shortages or key national needs, and providing student financial assistance in research and graduate training.

Finally, we concluded that the federal government has the primary responsibility to identify the national interest in education.

The Federal Response

Now that states and local jurisdictions have acted, now that it is clear from the national response to the education reports that major change is an important national priority, this is an especially appropriate time for those in the federal government to think about programmatic initiatives at the federal level that can complement and reinforce the educational reform movement. I note recent efforts by the Department of Education to make the results of educational research more easily available to professional educators and to policy makers.

Given the momentum that has been built up by the educational reform movement—and I believe it is altogether fair and accurate to say that much of the impetus for this could be attributed to the tireless efforts of former Secretary of Education T. H. Bell and the vigorous personal involvement of President Reagan—given that momentum, buttressed by the longstanding commitment you and your colleagues in the Congress have to help improve education in our country, systematic and complementary programmatic initiatives by the federal government will now have a far greater impact than they could have had even two years ago.

The Congress and the President now have a special opportunity to build on what has already been accomplished across the nation. I urge the federal government to move actively and confidently both to insure the reform movement's continuing success and to play its complementary role with the freshness of spirit and a sense of excitement fitted to this historic opportunity.

Looking Ahead

In thinking about the future of educational reform, one question seems to be of paramount importance; and I close with this comment. Can we sustain the momentum for change that has been created in the past few years? We are now at a turning point. We have accomplished a great deal in the first flush of enthusiasm. What remains is to incorporate reform as a lasting element in our school system—no easy task.

Can we move from the assumption that educational reform is something we do every 25 years, to the conviction that it is and ought to be a continuing effort? If we can't do that, then at the least we need five more years of sustained effort, the minimum, in my opinion, for lasting reform to take hold.

Can we summon the energy and the interest to follow through on so many promising beginnings? A central message of *A Nation at Risk* was that, if we truly care about our society, as indeed we do, our economy, our future as a country and as a free people, we will find a way to do so.

•

17 THE SOCIAL FOUNDATIONS OF EDUCATIONAL FAILURE

PROGRESS IS AN ILLUSION IN OUR EDUCATIONAL THIRD WORLD

Ernest L. Boyer

Ernest L. Boyer is the president of the Carnegie Foundation for the Advancement of Teaching and Senior Fellow at the Woodrow Wilson School, Princeton University, and was the former United States Commissioner of Education and Chancellor of the State University of New York.

Points to Consider:

1. What does the author mean by an "educational Third World"?
2. Why does the author suggest that federal leadership is necessary for Chapter I to succeed?
3. How will language serve as a dividing line in the United States?
4. Do you agree with the current moves to reform Chapter I? Why or why not?

Excerpted from testimony of Ernest L. Boyer before the House Subcommittee on Elementary, Secondary, and Vocational Education of the House Committee on Education and Labor, September 30, 1986.

What we could be left with in our major cities is a kind of educational Third World. And it is here, in these schools, that the battle of American education will be won or lost. If urban schools do not become a national priority, the promise of excellence in education will remain sadly unfulfilled.

Today much of the debate about school reform overflows with good news. We're told that schools are getting better without, they say, "another new federal program or an expansion of existing programs."

But what we're not being told is that while many "advantaged" schools seem to be improving, many others—especially those in our major cities—remain deeply troubled institutions. These schools differ not just in degree, but in kind. The social and economic problems that surround them are so great and the problems so complex that current efforts are just not adequate to the task.

Twenty years ago, there was a crusade in this nation to improve these troubled urban schools. The centerpiece was desegregation coupled with Title I of the Elementary and Secondary Education Act (now referred to as "Chapter I") and other compensatory education and nutritional programs. The crusade of the 1960s, now just a faded memory, has not been followed by new ideas or the full funding of those efforts which have, over the years, demonstrated their essential worth. Rather, in these difficult urban settings, we have seen a deepening of disillusionment and despair.

- In some city high schools, at least four out of ten students are absent on any given day. How are we to achieve excellence when students aren't even in the building?
- Almost half of the Mexican-American and Puerto Rican students who enroll in public schools drop out before they are awarded a diploma.
- In Philadelphia the drop out rate is 38 percent. And in Boston it's 43 percent.
- In Chicago, in 1984, over half of the students failed to graduate, and of those that did only a third were reading at the twelfth grade level.
- Last year in the Cleveland Public Schools there was not a single semi-finalist in the National Merit Scholarship competition. Boston and Detroit each had only *one* high school with semi-finalists.

Ernest L. Boyer, president of the Carnegie Foundation for the Advancement of Teaching and Senior Fellow at the Woodrow Wilson School, Princeton University.

The Educational Third World

While these failures have a secondary school focus—where, by the way, Chapter I funds are virtually absent—the truth is that the roots of these tragic statistics are in the earlier years. We're talking about children who can't read and write effectively, who cannot speak with clarity or listen with full understanding precisely because they have had a poor beginning. They are children who failed to receive—unfortunately and shamefully—the assistance needed at a time when it would have mattered most.

The harsh truth is that the school reform movement is not confronting adequately the core of our educational dilemma. And there remains an enormous gap between our rhetoric and results. The breakup of the home, the community wrenched by crime, lack of money, loss of good teachers—all of these threaten to overwhelm our most troubled schools. To require a failing student in an urban ghetto, for example, to take another unit in math or foreign language without a better climate or better teaching is like raising a hurdle without giving more coaching to someone who has already stumbled.

118

By the year 2000, America will be a nation in which one of every three pupils in the public schools will be non-white. What is coming toward the educational system is a group of children who will be poorer and more ethnically and linguistically diverse; children who will have more handicaps that surely will affect their schooling.

Unless we deepen our commitment, the crisis in urban education will increase. An aging white population will reduce support, and the gap will widen between the haves and the have-nots in education.

What we could be left with in our major cities is a kind of *educational Third World*. And it is here, in these schools, that the battle of American education will be won or lost. If urban schools do not become a national priority, the promise of excellence in education will remain sadly unfulfilled.

As we move toward the year 2000, the most urgent issue we confront is this: Will America continue to believe in education for all children or will it sort out schooling between the winners and the losers—and in so doing become a separated and more divided nation?

There is no simple answer to this challenge but I am convinced that Chapter I has a crucial role to play. And yet it's ironic that at the very moment the problem is increasing, support for this essential program has been going down.

In 1979, while I was Commissioner, we—even then—were getting Chapter I support to slightly fewer than half the children who qualified. Today, as I understand the data, only about 40 percent of those eligible are being served. And this decline has occurred at the very time the percentage of children in poverty has gone up. Since 1980 the percentage of children in poverty has, in fact, increased—from 16 percent to 21 percent today.

Chapter I—A Proven Program

I do not suggest that Chapter I, even if fully funded, will be sufficient. It is, however, a proven program and, if better funded, could give large numbers of disadvantaged children a much better start. Further, if Chapter I does not become a national priority, the promise of excellence will remain sadly unfulfilled.

In recent years Chapter I has become far less regulatory with states and schools now having more flexibility in the kinds of programs they can offer. In spite of the "deregulation," however, very little has changed in practices at the local school. The patterns established in the late 1960s and 1970s— teacher aids, pull-out programs, direct instruction in discrete skills in reading and math, using mostly elementary, basic materials—continue to dominate.

The lack of change suggests to me the need for federal leadership, efforts to help school districts think larger about the possibilities, including after school programs and summer programs of greater consequence, programs that are richer in their language base, that take development more seriously through ungraded primary systems, and the like. I would hope that such leadership has not been compromised by the efforts to deregulate many aspects of Chapter I.

A shift in regulations that has, unfortunately, made a large difference relates to parents. With the end of the requirement for Parent Advisory Councils, parental involvement in Chapter I has declined dramatically. That is not a change I can applaud.

When I became Commissioner of Education, I soon was convinced that Chapter I is an absolutely crucial program that reflects the essence of what the federal partnership is all about, because it strikes at the heart of equity in education, which I think is a constitutional and moral mandate.

That conviction has deepened in the years since I have left federal service, simply because the need has increased and because the issue of literacy, not only among children but among adults, has become so crucial to the economic and social and civic vitality of this nation . . . .

We've had in recent months tremendous publicity surrounding adult illiteracy. The recent National Assessment of Educational Progress (NAEP) report indicates that while most of our young adults can recognize words—they are literate in a technical sense—they are not literate in understanding meaning and in using subtle language which, I think, is increasingly crucial in our sophisticated culture . . . .

As I look down the road, I see the nation divided not just on the basis of rich or poor or geographically. I see language being the great dividing line; that is, those who are linguistically empowered and can use symbols and engage economically and civicly in the work of this nation. And on the other side of that dividing line, those who are not effective in the use of English, who cannot engage in the discourse of this country, and who cannot even be productively employed.

Unless we find a way to close the gap between those who understand and use language effectively and those who remain linguistically impoverished, I believe the future of the nation is imperiled . . . .

Here then is my conclusion. I think we face a dramatic illiteracy problem in this nation. My only hope is in the long-term belief that, if we can tackle it in the early years when the readiness for learning is greatest, if we can provide compensatory help especially around the empowerment for language when children learn language best, then I believe we will start cashing in on improvement for the future. And if we do not do that, then I'm afraid, given the demography, the problem of illiteracy and lack of empowerment geometrically will increase, and this nation will become a weakened and divided nation.

Language Development

Since this hearing connects Chapter I to literacy, I'd like to say something more about the essentialness of language. I'm convinced that language is the centerpiece of effective education. While we have in this country serious literacy problems among adults, the best means of assuring that these problems are not duplicated in each succeeding generation is to focus on the early years. If young children gain a fundamental grasp of language, their social and educational prospects are enormously enhanced. If they do not become proficient in English, it is almost impossible to fully compensate for the failure later on.

Chapter I, imaginatively organized and adequately funded, should be targeted even more directly on language development. This means, for me, school settings where children speak, where teachers read from the vast storehouse of children's literature and provide them opportunities to hear a rich array of words used in many different contexts. It means settings where children write from the beginning of their schooling, and where quality books become the standard fare.

Secretary Bennet said it right in *First Lessons* when he described too many classrooms that are silent, where children sit all day working through "skill sheets" that have little to do with language, and use textbooks that keep them from literature that has the potential to enrich language possibilities.

And the governors were even more right when they said that the early years, especially with regard to issues of language, were so important that class sizes should be limited to 15 students.

Revise Chapter I?

Before closing, I must say something about current moves to revise Chapter I. As I last read *The Equity and Choice Act,* parents of eligible children would receive a voucher that could be used at a public school in the same district, at a public school in another district, or at a private school. The argument is that making billions of dollars available to parents would create a demand for services and the free market would quickly supply a wide range of programs superior to those that currently exist.

Frankly, I'm skeptical of this proposal. What will the choices really be for the students with a $500 or $600 voucher? A student in Detroit wishing to go to a public elementary school in Grossè Pointe would face a huge nonresidential tuition bill— assuming that Grosse Pointe is willing to take on the student. With the existing private schools also beyond reach, and parochial schools likely out for constitutional reasons, what are the real choices?

I'm afraid a large number of entrepreneurial "tutoring schools" of the fast food variety would crop up while the modest enrichment programs in the nation's already beleaguered inner city schools would be further undermined. To put it frankly, we would be dismantling a proven program in the name of school reform with no well structured, high quality program to replace it. The time has come to reaffirm the federal partnership in education, not dilute it.

18 THE SOCIAL FOUNDATIONS OF EDUCATIONAL FAILURE

EDUCATION HAS ERODED MORAL VALUES

Elaine Andreski

Elaine Andreski is a citizen who came to testify before the House Sub-committee on Elementary, Secondary, and Vocational Education about the educational shortcomings of her local school district and the problems her children faced.

Points to Consider:

1. What rights do parents have in protesting school curriculum?
2. How did the author handle the education of her two youngest children?
3. What features of American education does the author disagree with?
4. Does the author support the Elementary and Secondary Education Act? Why or why not?

Excerpted from testimony of Elaine Andreski before the House Sub-committee on Elementary, Secondary, and Vocational Education of the House Committee on Education and Labor, March 20, 1986.

Remember, a nation cannot remain free and illiterate at the same time. Parents must regain control over their children and the institutions they support to teach their offspring.

Nothing in the records of history has reached the deplorable situation we as a people are faced with as the problems of illiteracy, destruction of traditional values, and violence that reflect the social change promoted by our educators over the past 30 years or so. As a parent of four children, all grown now, and as a parent activist for almost 20 years, I have witnessed firsthand most of what my testimony includes. While my two older children have been "cheated" by the government schools, I must confess that I chose to take the situation into my own hands in 1977 by homeschooling the two younger ones. They are both working full time after their graduation from our home school and are presently attending Macomb County College on a part-time basis. My traditional Roman Catholic religious beliefs demanded no less from me.

Parental Rights

In 1975 Kenneth A. Schuylman, a member of the St. Johns Law Review and the St. Thomas More Institute for Legal Research, wrote a research paper entitled *Parental Control of Public School Curriculum.* The study focused in on parents' rights and where the line could be drawn regarding protests of curriculum. The report goes on to say, "It is well established that a parent cannot successfully avail himself of the use of the courts simply on the basis of a disagreement he may have with the curriculum as prescribed by the board of education or the state. The Supreme Court has clearly pointed out that, 'Courts do not and cannot intervene in the resolution of conflicts which arise in the daily operation of school systems and which do not directly and sharply implicate basic constitutional values. It may be concluded, therefore, that parents will fail in their challenges if their criticisms do not reach constitutional proportions or the constitutional infringement is justified by a greater state interest.'

"Even where these constitutional rights have been violated, parents have still been denied the right to control the education of their children where a court finds that the state's interest in directing education is superior.

"Unless they resort to private schools or more effectively influence the public school boards on election day, the dissatisfied parents...will find that the right to control the education of their child stops at the school house gate."

Failure of American Schools

The American educational system used to be the finest in the world. It trained young people to become useful and productive citizens, transmitting the values and standards of our forefathers to the younger generation.

The incredible sum of tax monies Americans have poured into the system in recent years has resulted in poor test results, with scholastic aptitude tests declining every year for the past 18 years. Diplomas are granted to students who cannot read, write, spell, and do simple math problems. Many experts believe our system has been sabotaged. Our children have been defrauded of the basic tools of learning for which the parents paid a terrible price.

In far too many schools pupils are taught only what is wrong with America, discounting the fact that this benevolent nation has donated billions of dollars to feed the hungry, clothe the naked, and educate others, earning us the nickname, "breadbasket of the world." And our own criticize us for not having done enough. The truth is that our system has provided more political freedom and economic abundance to more people than any other nation in the world.

Aside from condemning our country, the failure to teach basic skills and fundamental truths has left a void that was ultimately filled with values clarification, a system of probing and changing the child's values by techniques such as violent and disturbing books, films, and materials dealing with parental conflict, running away, death, drugs, murder, suicide, mental illness, poverty, despair, and anger or by requiring the child to engage in role playing of death, pregnancy, abortion, anger, suicide, and hate.

Personal evaluations and surveys which invade the private thoughts and acts of the child and his family are randomly used in whatever classes are found suitable. The deliberate attempt to make a child question his parents' values via values clarification drives a psychological

125

wedge between parent and child, while the latter adopts an autonomy unbeknown to that particular age group.

For the last 25 years, protests have been conducted on every scale imaginable from the four corners of the United States. Parents, who have tried to sue the school system in New York for malpractice, found themselves thrown out of court. Their son had graduated from high school an illiterate.

The 1970s and 1980s have ushered in, first, the religion of secular humanism as a philosophical base for our public school children, and second, the Eastern occult—Hindu practices such as meditation, yoga, and guided imagery as a means of reducing stress and improving motivation.

In other words, our present-day system of education has been reduced to a laboratory of behavorial psychology, using stimulus and response techniques that originally were used on dogs, rats, and chickens. Operant conditioning, fathered by B. F. Skinner, the social engineer, has been adapted by almost every school in America. . . .

Ineffective Legislation

For parents who were alerted to these dangers long ago, what became known as the Hatch Amendment was finally a vehicle or tool to be used to put an end to the experiments being conducted on a captive audience, the school children of America. The change agents who boast of radically altering the morals and values of our children could finally be confronted.

"In 1965 Congress gave the notorious National Education Association (NEA) what it wanted, the Elementary and Secondary Education Act, a virtual key to the federal treasury," says Sam Blumenfeld in *NEA: Trojan Horse in American Education.* This bill was originally created for the alleged purpose of compensatory educational programs for the "emotionally disadvantaged," Title I. However, it also created many other categorical programs providing funding for such things as library services, Title II; exemplary elementary and secondary school programs (experimental programs), Title III; state departments of education, Title V; and bilingual education, Title VII.

Almost immediately government publications, such as *Pacesetters in Innovation,* became available that would change the approach to education from the cognitive (intellect) area to the affective (feelings and emotions) area, which is behavioral in nature. The phenomenal growth of federal intrusion began to be felt from coast to coast, but few parents had even the faintest idea of the revolution taking place. The pacesetters' direction was to organize the process of change to reorganize and restructure the entire school system. Teachers were subject to sensitivity training and change agents training through in-service training, not only to condition the teachers to new philosophies, but to spread their influence to others in their own districts and throughout the state by way of various visitation programs.

The result was structured and graded classes being systematically phased out and replaced by ungraded, individualized instruction (B-STEP), subject to a preconceived mold or norm by computerized assessment called PPBS (National Curriculum). The teacher then became a facilitator or clinician, monitoring the cycling and recycling of attitudinal changes in the student.

A lone voice in Congress, that of the Honorable Earl F. Landgrebe, a congressman from Indiana, voiced his objection to the extension of the Elementary and Secondary Education Act (the Act) that would carry it through 1978. His pleas were ignored as he raised four crucial issues that were never addressed: 1. federal control, 2. parental rights, 3. content of educational programs, and 4. the results of such. An evaluation was conducted by the American Institute for Research (AIR) in March 1972 and concluded that participants in Title I programs gained less during the period of instruction than nonparticipants and consequently fell further behind their non-participants (non-federally funded) peers and national norms. Other studies also indicated that the $13 billion spent under the Act had not resulted in any educational improvement. Since its effectiveness as a federal program had failed, Congressman Landgrebe proposed HR10639 to phase out the Act within four years and to grant local control to school districts once again, prohibiting psychotherapy techniques, forcing teacher membership in unions, and restricting title programs to the cognitive area only.

It was not surprising that his bill did not pass, but one man alone is no match for the socialist majority in the legislature. The courageous lawmaker from Indiana was defeated in his fourth bid for office and the American people experienced a terrible loss.

A brief attempt was made to rid our schools of experimental programs with the introduction of the Hatch Amendment (1978), but because no regulations were issued at this time, it proved to be an ineffective piece of legislation, not worth the paper it was printed on. Since that time, regulations have been issued, but the final rules exclude any professional input regarding complaints against federal programs. Since nonacademic courses are the only programs affected, the academic courses will be immune from prosecution and teachers can have a field day in such classes. This amounts to a slap in the face of all those parents who traveled great distances at their own expense to testify at the Hatch hearings.

The damage done to the teaching profession can only be repaired by the teachers themselves now, by upgrading their own standards of character and rebelling against their own leadership. Teachers claim they are victims of abuse, yet they fail to recognize that parents were the first victims of educational battle fatigue—for us there was no place to turn for help.

I would like to conclude this testimony by asking you to assist Senator Zorinsky by supporting his legislation, the National Commission on Illiteracy Act. Timing is crucial; we've got no time to lose. Millions of young people have already been affected and our country cannot afford any more twisted minds. Since reading lies at the heart of all learning, this is an excellent place to start.

Final Plea

Remember, a nation cannot remain free and illiterate at the same time. Parents must regain control over their children and the institutions they support to teach their offspring. James J. Kilpatrick, the conservative columnist, wrote in a 1978 column, "I get angry letters from parents about these bizarre incidents, but I don't get nearly enough angry letters. Parents are too docile, dumb, or brainwashed. We ought to get mad at the behavioral boys who would cure our children of nonexistent illnesses. And we ought to stay mad." I couldn't agree with him more.

19 THE SOCIAL FOUNDATIONS OF EDUCATIONAL FAILURE

CULTURAL ILLITERACY: UNDERMINING THE SOCIAL FOUNDATIONS OF EDUCATION

E. D. Hirsch, Jr.

E. D. Hirsch, Jr., is William R. Kenan Professor of English at the University of Virginia and is the author of Cultural Literacy: What Every American Needs to Know. *His articles on cultural literacy have appeared in the* New York Times Education Supplement, The American Scholar, *and* American Educator, *and he frequently speaks on the subject. Dr. Hirsch is a member of the American Academy of Arts and Sciences, has been a Senior Fellow of the National Endowment for the Humanities, and is a member of the federally sponsored Foundation of Literacy project.*

Points to Consider:

1. How does the author define "cultural literacy"?
2. Why have large U.S. companies, including CBS and Exxon, made a grant to the American Academy of Arts and Sciences?
3. How many American seventeen-year-olds were unable to identify either Stalin or Churchill?
4. Why has the need for cultural literacy been rarely mentioned in discussions of education?
5. In what grades does the author recommend instruction in the literate national culture?

Cultural literacy lies above the everyday levels of knowledge that everyone possesses and below the expert level known only to specialists. It is that middle ground of cultural knowledge possessed by the "common reader." It includes information that we have traditionally expected our children to receive in school, but which they no longer do.

To be culturally literate is to possess the basic information needed to thrive in the modern world. The breadth of that information is great, extending over the major domains of human activity from sports to science. It is by no means confined to "culture" narrowly understood as an acquaintance with the arts. Nor is it confined to one social class. Quite the contrary. Cultural literacy constitutes the only sure avenue of opportunity for disadvantaged children, the only reliable way of combating the social determinism that now condemns them to remain in the same social and educational condition as their parents. That children from poor and illiterate homes tend to remain poor and illiterate is an unacceptable failure of our schools, one which has occurred not because our teachers are inept but chiefly because they are compelled to teach a fragmented curriculum based on faulty educational theories. Some say that our schools by themselves are powerless to change the cycle of poverty and illiteracy. I do not agree. They can break the cycle, but only if they themselves break fundamentally with some of the theories and practices that education professors and school administrators have followed over the past fifty years. . . .

The Decline of Literate Knowledge

The standard of literacy required by modern society has been rising throughout the developed world, but American literacy rates have not risen to meet this standard. What seemed an acceptable level in the 1950s is no longer acceptable in the late 1980s, when only highly literate societies can prosper economically. Much of Japan's industrial efficiency has been credited to its almost universally high level of literacy. But in the United States, only two thirds of our citizens are literate, and even among those the average level is too low and should be raised. The remaining third of our citizens need to be brought as close to true literacy as possible. Ultimately our aim should be to attain universal literacy at a very high level, to achieve not only greater economic prosperity but also greater social justice and more effective democracy. We Americans have long accepted literacy as a paramount aim of schooling, but only recently have some of us who have done research in the field begun

A DEFINITION

Students read more fluently and with greater understanding if they have background knowledge of the past and present. Such knowledge and understanding is called cultural literacy.

U.S. Department of Education, What Works: Research About Teaching and Learning, *1986*

to realize that literacy is far more than a skill and that it requires large amounts of specific information. . . .

Professor Jeanne S. Chall is one of several reading specialists who have observed that "world knowledge" is essential to the development of reading and writing skills.[1] What she calls world knowledge I call cultural literacy, namely, the network of information that all competent readers possess. It is the background information, stored in their minds, that enables them to take up a newspaper and read it with an adequate level of comprehension, getting the point, grasping the implications, relating what they read to the unstated context which alone gives meaning to what they read. In describing the contents of this neglected domain of background information, I try to direct attention to a new opening that can help our schools make the significant improvement in education that has so far eluded us. The achievement of high universal literacy is the key to all other fundamental improvements in American education.

Why is literacy so important in the modern world? Some of the reasons, like the need to fill out forms or get a good job, are so obvious that they needn't be discussed. But the chief reason is broader. The complex undertakings of modern life depend on the cooperation of many people with different specialities in different places. Where communications fail, so do the undertakings. (That is the moral of the story of the Tower of Babel.) The function of national literacy is to foster effective nationwide communications. Our chief instrument of communication over time and space is the standard national language, which is sustained by national literacy. Mature literacy alone enables the tower to be built, the business to be well managed, and the airplane to fly without crashing. All nationwide communications, whether by telephone, radio, TV, or writing are fundamentally dependent upon literacy, for the essence of literacy is not simply reading and writing but also the effective use of the standard literate language. In Spain and most of Latin America the literate language is standard written Spanish. In Japan it is standard written Japanese. In our country it is standard written English. . . .

132

In *Cultural Literacy,* Dr. E.D. Hirsch calls for a new emphasis on information in education.

The recently rediscovered insight that literacy is more than a skill is based upon knowledge that all of us unconsciously have about language. We know instinctively that to understand what somebody is saying, we must understand more than the surface meanings of words; we have to understand the context as well. The need for background information applies all the more to reading and writing. To grasp the words on a page we have to know a lot of information that isn't set down on the page. . . .

In order to put in perspective the importance of background knowledge in language, I want to connect the lack of it with our recent lack of success in teaching mature literacy to all students. The most broadly based evidence about our teaching of literacy comes from the National Assessment of Educational Progress (NAEP). This nationwide measurement, mandated by Congress, shows that between 1970 and 1980 seventeen-year-olds declined in their ability to understand written materials, and the decline was especially striking in the top group, those able to read at an "advanced" level.[2] Although these scores have now begun to rise, they remain alarmingly low. Still more precise quantitative data have come from the scores of the verbal Scholastic Aptitude Test (SAT). According to John B. Carroll, a distinguished psychometrician, the verbal SAT is essentially a test of "advanced vocabulary knowledge," which makes it a fairly sensitive instrument for measuring levels of literacy.[3] It is well known that verbal SAT scores have declined dramatically in the past fifteen years, and though recent reports have shown them rising again, it is from a very low base. Moreover, performance on the verbal SAT has been slipping steadily *at the top.* Ever fewer numbers of our best and brightest students are making high scores on the test. . . .

In the mid 1980s American business leaders have become alarmed by the lack of communication skills in the young people they employ. Recently, top executives of some large U.S. companies, including CBS and Exxon, met to discuss the fact that their younger middle-level executives could no longer communicate their ideas effectively in speech or writing. This group of companies has made a grant to the American Academy of Arts and Sciences to analyze the causes of this growing problem. They want to know why, despite breathtaking advances in the technology of communication, the effectiveness of business communication has been slipping, to the detriment of our competitiveness in the world. The figures from NAEP surveys and the scores on the verbal SAT are solid evidence that literacy has been declining in this country just when our need for effective literacy has been sharply rising.

I now want to juxtapose some evidence for another kind of educational decline, one that is related to the drop in literacy. During the period 1970-1985, the amount of shared knowledge that we have been able to take for granted in communicating with our fellow citizens has also been declining. More and more of our young people don't know things we used to assume they knew. . . . Like every other human group they share a tremendous amount of knowledge among themselves, much of it learned in school. The trouble is that, from the standpoint of their literacy and their ability to communicate with others in our culture, what they know is short-lived, and narrowly confined to their own generation. Many young people strikingly lack the information that writers of American books and newspapers have traditionally taken for granted among their readers from all generations. Our children's lack of intergenerational information is a serious problem for the nation. The decline of literacy and the decline of shared knowledge are closely related, interdependent facts.

The evidence for the decline of shared knowledge is not just anecdotal. . . .The Foundations of Literacy project is measuring some of the specific information about history and literature that American seventeen-year-olds possess.

Although the full report will not be published until 1987, the preliminary field tests are disturbing.[4] If these samplings hold up, and there is no reason to think they will not, then the results we will be reading in 1987 will show that two thirds of our seventeen-year-olds do not know that the Civil War occurred between 1850 and 1900. Three quarters do not know what *reconstruction* means. Half do not know the meaning of *Brown decision* and cannot identify either Stalin or Churchill. Three quarters are unfamiliar with the names of standard American and British authors. Moreover, our seventeen-year-olds have little sense of geography or the relative chronology of major events. Reports of youthful ignorance can no longer be considered merely impressionistic[5] . . . .

The Nature and Use of Cultural Literacy

The documented decline in shared knowledge carries implications that extend to larger questions of educational policy and social justice in our country. Mina Shaughnessy was a great English teacher who devoted her professional life to helping disadvantaged students become literate. At the 1980 conference dedicated to her memory, one of the speakers who followed me to the podium was the Harvard historian and sociologist Orlando Patterson. To my delight he departed from his prepared talk to mention mine. He seconded my argument that shared information is a necessary background to true literacy. Then he extended and deepened the ideas I had presented. Here is what Professor Patterson said, as reported in the *Proceedings* of the conference.

Industrialized civilization [imposes] a growing cultural and structural complexity which requires persons to have a broad grasp of what Professor Hirsch has called cultural literacy: a deep understanding of mainstream culture, which no longer has much to do with white Anglo-Saxon Protestants, but with the imperatives of industrial civilization. It is the need for cultural literacy, a profound conception of the whole civilization, which is often neglected in talk about literacy.

Patterson continued by drawing a connection between background information and the ability to hold positions of responsibility and power. He was particularly concerned with the importance for blacks and other minorities of possessing this information, which is essential for improving their social and economic status.

> The people who run society at the macro-level must be literate in this culture. For this reason, it is dangerous to overemphasize the problems of basic literacy or the relevancy of literacy to specific tasks, and more constructive to emphasize that blacks will be condemned in perpetuity to oversimplified, low-level tasks and will never gain their rightful place in controlling the levers of power unless they also acquire literacy in this wider cultural sense.

Although Patterson focused his remarks on the importance of cultural literacy for minorities, his observations hold for every culturally illiterate person in our nation. Indeed, as he observed, cultural literacy is not the property of any group or class.

> To assume that this wider culture is static is an error; in fact it is not. It's not a WASP culture; it doesn't belong to any group. It is essentially and constantly changing, and it is open. What is needed is recognition that the accurate metaphor or model for this wider literacy is not domination, but dialectic; each group participates and contributes, transforms and is transformed, as much as any other group. . . .The English language no longer belongs to any single group or nation. The same goes for any other area of the wider culture.[6]

As Professor Patterson suggested, being taught to decode elementary reading materials and specific, job-related texts cannot constitute true literacy. Such basic training does not make a person literate with respect to newspapers or other writings addressed to a general public. Moreover, a directly practical drawback of such narrow training is that it does not prepare anyone for technological change. Narrow vocational training in one state of a technology will not enable a person to read manuals that explain new developments in the same technology. In modern life we need general knowledge that enables us to deal with new ideas, events, and challenges. In today's world, general cultural literacy is more useful than what Professor Patterson terms "literacy to a specific task," because general literate information is the basis for many changing tasks.

Cultural literacy is even more important in the social sphere. The aim of universal literacy has never been a socially neutral mission in our country. Our traditional social goals were unforgettably renewed for us by Martin Luther King, Jr., in his "I Have a Dream" speech. King envisioned a country where the children of former slaves sit down at the table of equality with the children of former slave owners, where men and women deal with each other as equals and judge each other on their characters and achievements rather than their origins. Like Thomas Jefferson, he had a dream of a society founded not on race or class but on personal merit.

In present day, that dream depends on mature literacy. No modern society can hope to become a just society without a high level of universal literacy. Putting aside for the moment the practical arguments about the economic uses of literacy, we can contemplate the even more basic principle that underlies our national system of education in the first place—that people in a democracy can be entrusted to decide all important matters for themselves because they can deliberate and communicate with one another. Universal literacy is inseparable from democracy and is the canvas for Martin Luther King's picture as well as for Thomas Jefferson's.

Both of these leaders understood that having the right to vote is meaningless if a citizen is disenfranchised by illiteracy or semiliteracy. Illiterate and semiliterate Americans are condemned not only to poverty, but also to the powerlessness of incomprehension. Knowing that they do not understand the issues, and feeling prey to manipulative oversimplifications, they do not trust the system of which they are supposed to be the masters. They do not feel themselves to be active participants in our republic, and they often do not turn out to vote. The civic importance of cultural literacy lies in the fact that true enfranchisement depends upon knowledge, knowledge upon literacy, and literacy upon cultural literacy.

To be truly literate, citizens must be able to grasp the meaning of any piece of writing addressed to the general reader. All citizens should be able, for instance, to read newspapers of substance, about which Jefferson made the following famous remark:

> Were it left to me to decide whether we should have a government without newspapers, or newspapers without a government, I should not hesitate a moment to prefer the latter. But I should mean that every man should receive those papers and be capable of reading them.[7]

Jefferson's last comment is often omitted when the passage is quoted, but it's the crucial one.

Books and newspapers assume a "common reader," that is, a person who knows the things known by other literate persons in the culture. Obviously, such assumptions are never identical from writer to writer, but they show a remarkable consistency. Those who write for a mass public are always making judgments about what their readers can be assumed to know, and the judgments are closely similar. Any reader who doesn't possess the knowledge assumed in a piece he or she reads will in fact be illiterate with respect to that particular piece of writing . . . .

Although nationalism may be regrettable in some of its worldwide political effects, a mastery of national culture is essential to mastery of the standard language in every modern nation. This point is important for educational policy, because educators often stress the virtues of multicultural education. Such study is indeed valuable in itself; it instills tolerance and provides a perspective on our own traditions and values. But however laudable it is, it should not be the primary focus of national education. It should not be allowed to supplant or interfere with our schools' responsibility to ensure our children's mastery of American literate culture. The acculturative responsibility of the schools is primary and fundamental. To teach the ways of one's own community has always been and still remains the essence of the education of our children, who enter neither a narrow tribal culture nor a transcendent world culture but a national literate culture. For profound historical reasons, this is the way of the modern world.[8] It will not change soon, and it will certainly not be changed by educational policy alone.

The Decline of Teaching Cultural Literacy

Why have our schools failed to fulfill their fundamental acculturative responsibility? In view of the immense importance of cultural literacy for speaking, listening, reading, and writing, why has the need for a definite, shared body of information been so rarely mentioned in discussions of education? . . .

Let me hazard a guess about one reason for our neglect of the subject. We have ignored cultural literacy in thinking about education—certainly I as a researcher also ignored it until recently—precisely because it was something we have been able to take for granted. We ignore the air we breathe until it is thin or foul. Cultural literacy is the oxygen of social intercourse. Only when we run into cultural illiteracy are we shocked into recognizing the importance of the information that we had unconsciously assumed.

To be sure, a minimal level of information is possessed by any normal person who lives in the United States and speaks elementary English. Almost everybody knows what is meant by *dollar* and that cars must travel on the right-hand side of the road. But this elementary level of information is not sufficient for a modern democracy. It isn't sufficient to read newspapers (a sin against Jeffersonian democracy), and it isn't sufficient to achieve economic fairness and high productivity. Cultural literacy lies *above* the everyday levels of knowledge that everyone possesses and *below* the expert level known only to specialists. It is that middle ground of cultural knowledge possessed by the "common reader." It includes information that we have traditionally expected our children to receive in school, but which they no longer do. . . .

It will not do to blame television for the state of our literacy. Television watching does reduce reading and often encroaches on homework. Much of it is admittedly the intellectual equivalent of junk food. But in some respects, such as its use of standard written English, television watching is acculturative.[9] Moreover, as Herbert Walberg points out, the schools themselves must be held partly responsible for excessive television watching, because they have not firmly insisted that students complete significant amounts of homework, an obvious way to increase time spent on reading and writing.[10] Nor should our schools be excused by an appeal to the effects of the decline of the family or the vicious circle of poverty, important as these factors are. Schools have, or should have, children for six or seven hours a day, five days a week, nine months a year, for thirteen years or more. To assert that they are powerless to make a significant impact on what their students learn would be to make a claim about American education that few parents, teachers, or students would find it easy to accept. . . .

The failure of our schools to create a literate society is sometimes excused on the grounds that the schools have been asked to do too much. They are asked, for example, to pay due regard to the demands of both local and national acculturation. They are asked to teach not only American history but also state and city history, driving, cardio-pulmonary resuscitation, consumerism, carpentry, cooking, and other special subjects. They are given the task of teaching information that is sometimes too rudimentary and sometimes too specialized. If the schools did not undertake this instruction, much of the information so provided would no doubt go unlearned. In some of our national moods we would like the schools to teach everything, but they cannot. There is a pressing need for clarity about our educational priorities. . . .

The concept of cultural literacy helps us to make such decisions because it places a higher value on national than on local information. We want to make our children competent to communicate with Americans throughout the land. . . .

The Critical Importance of Early Schooling

Once we become aware of the inherent connection between literacy and cultural literacy, we have a duty to those who lack cultural literacy to determine and disclose its contents. To someone who is unaware of the things a literate person is expected to know, a writer's assumption that readers possess cultural literacy could appear to be a conspiracy of the literate against the illiterate, for the purpose of keeping them out of the club. But there is no conspiracy. Writers *must* make assumptions about the body of information their readers know. Unfortunately for the disadvantaged, no one ever spells out what that information is. . . .

Preschool is not too early for starting earnest instruction in literate national culture. Fifth grade is almost too late. Tenth grade usually is too late. Anyone who is skeptical of this assertion should take a look at a heterogeneous class of fifth-graders engaged in summarizing a piece they have read. There are predictable differences between the summaries given by children with culturally adequate backgrounds and those given by children without. Although disadvantaged children often show an acceptable ability to decode and pronounce individual words, they are frequently unable to gain an integrated sense of a piece as a whole. They miss central implications and associations because they don't possess the background knowledge necessary to put the text into context. Hearing they hear not, and seeing they do not understand[11]. . . .

The importance of this evidence for improving our national literacy can scarcely be overemphasized. If in the early grades our children were taught texts with cultural content rather than "developmental" texts that develop abstract skills, much of the specific knowledge deficit of disadvantaged children could be overcome. For it is clear that one critical difference in the reading performances of disadvantaged fifth-graders as compared with advantaged pupils is the difference in their cultural knowledge. Background knowledge does not take care of itself. Reading and writing are cumulative skills; the more we read the more necessary knowledge we gain for further reading . . . .

Really effective reforms in the teaching of cultural literacy must therefore begin with the earliest grades. Every improvement made in teaching very young children literate background information will have a multiplier effect on later learning, not just by virtue of the information they will gain but also by virtue of the greater motivation for reading and learning they will feel when they actually understand what they have read.

---

[1] For rising standards of literacy, see R. L. Thorndike, *Reading Comprehension Education in Fifteen Countries: An Empirical Study* (New York: Wiley, 1973). On the connection between high literacy and Japan's economic performance, see Thomas P. Rohlen, "Japanese Education: If They Can Do It, Should We?" *American Scholar* 55, I (Winter 1985-86): 29-44. For American literacy rates see Jeanne Chall, "Afterword," in R. C. Anderson et al., *Becoming a Nation of Readers: The Report of the Commission on Reading* (Washington, D. C.: National Institute of Education, 1985), 123-24. On "world knowledge" in literacy, see Jeanne S. Chall, *Stages of Reading Development* (New York: McGraw-Hill, 1983), 8.

[2] National Assessment of Educational Progress, *Three National Assessments of Reading: Changes in Performance, 1970-1980* (Report II-R-OI) (Denver: Education Commission of the States, 1981). The percentage of students scoring at the "advanced" level (4.9 percent) has climbed back to the very low levels of 1970. See *The Reading Report Card: Progress Toward Excellence in Our Schools, Trends in Reading Over Four National Assessments, 1971-1984* (Princeton, N.J.: Educational Testing Service No. 15-R-OI, 1986).

3 John B. Carroll, "Psychometric Approaches to the Study of Language Abilities," in C. J. Fillmore, D. Kempler, and S.-Y. Wang, eds., *Individual Differences in Language Abilities and Language Behavior* (New York: Academic Press, 1979).

4 The Foundations of Literacy Project under a grant from the National Endowment for the Humanities, has commissioned NAEP, now conducted by the Educational Testing Service of Princeton, to probe the literary and historical knowledge of American seventeen-year-olds.

5 I am breaking no confidences as a member of the NAEP panel in revealing these pretest figures. They were made public on October 8, 1985, in a press release by NEH Chairman John Agresto, which stated in part: "Preliminary findings indicate that two-thirds of the seventeen-year-old students tested could not place the Civil War in the correct half century; a third did not know that the Declaration of Independence was signed between 1750 and 1800; half could not locate the half century in which the First World War occurred; a third did not know that Columbus sailed for the New World 'before 1750'; three-fourths could not identify Walt Whitman or Thoreau or E. E. Cummings or Carl Sandburg. And one-half of our high school seniors did not recognize the names of Winston Churchill or Joseph Stalin."

6 Orlando Patterson, "Language, Ethnicity, and Change," in S. G. D'Eloia, ed., *Toward a Literate Democracy: Proceedings of the First Shaughnessy Memorial Conference, April 3, 1980,* special number of *The Journal of Basic Writing III* (1980); 72-73.

7 Letter to Colonel Edward Carrington, January 16, 1787, taken from *The Life and Selected Writings of Thomas Jefferson,* ed. A. Koch and W. Peden (New York: Random House, 1944), 411-12.

8 This is fully discusssed in Chapter 3 of *Cultural Literacy.*

9 "Up to about ten hours a week, there is actually a slight positive relationship between the amount of time children spend watching TV and their school achievement, including reading achievement. Beyond this point, the relationship turns negative and, as the number of hours per week climbs, achievement declines sharply." R. C. Anderson et al., *Becoming a Nation of Readers,* 27.

10 Walberg and Shanahan, "High School Effects on Individual Students," 4-9.

11 Jeanne S. Chall, "Afterword," in R. C. Anderson et al., *Becoming a National of Readers,* 123-25.

INTERPRETING
EDITORIAL CARTOONS

This activity may be used an an individualized study guide for students in libraries and resource centers or as a discussion catalyst in small group and classroom discussions.

Although cartoons are usually humorous, the main intent of most political cartoonists is not to entertain. Cartoons express serious social comment about important issues. Using graphics and visual arts, the cartoonist expresses opinions and attitudes. By employing an entertaining and often light-hearted visual format, cartoonists may have as much or more impact on national and world issues as editorial and syndicated columnists.

Points to Consider:

1. Examine the cartoon in this activity. (See next page.)

2. How would you describe the message of this cartoon? Try to describe the message in one to three sentences.

3. Do you agree with the message expressed in this cartoon? Why or why not?

4. Does the cartoon support the author's point of view in any of the readings in this book? If the answer is yes, be specific about which reading or readings and why.

5. Are any of the readings in chapter three in basic agreement with this cartoon?

BIBLIOGRAPHY

A Nation at Risk: The Imperative for Educational Reform. Report to the Nation and to the Secretary of Education by the National Commission on Excellence, April 1983.

Anderson, Richard. *Hearings on Language and Literacy before the National Commission on Excellence in Education,* Staff Summary. Houston: April 16, 1982.

Artley, Sterl A. Foreword. In William S. Gray, *On Their Own in Reading.* Cited in Mitford Mathew, *Teaching to Read;* Chicago: University of Chicago Press, 1966.

Aukerman, Robert G. *Reading in the Secondary School Classroom.* New York: McGraw-Hill Book Company, 1972.

Background Information Bulletin. The International Reading Association, Newark, Delaware, 1980.

Beck, Joan. "Scientists Tag 'Can't Read' Gene." *The Chicago Tribune,* March 23, 1983.

Beck, Isabell and Ellen S. McCaslin. *An Analysis of Dimensions that Effect the Development of Code-Breaking Ability in Eight Beginning Reading Programs.* University of Pittsburgh, Learning Research and Development Center, 1978.

Bhola, H. S. "The Elusive Goal of World Literacy." *Development Communication Report,* April 1980.

Bond, Guy L. and Miles A. Tinker. *Reading Difficulties: Their Diagnosis and Correction.* New York: Appleton-Century-Crofts, 1967.

Brown, Rexford. "Literacy Is Not So Basic." *Compact,* Fall 1981, pp. 16–19.

Brunner, Michael. "Adult Illiteracy and School Instruction." Paper prepared for the National Advisory Council on Adult Education, 1983.

Chall, Jeanne S. *Learning to Read: The Great Debate.* (Updated version). New York: McGraw-Hill, 1983.

Chall, Jeanne S. "Literacy: Trends and Explanations." *Educational Researcher, 12,* No. 9, November 1983.

Copperman, Paul. *The Literacy Hoax.* New York: William Morrow and Co., 1978.

Darling, Sharon. *Final Report.* Jefferson County Adult Reading Project, Department of Adult and Continuing Education, Jefferson County Board of Education. Louisville, Kentucky: June 1981.

Developing High School Reading Programs. Edited by Mildred A. Dawson. Newark, Delaware: International Reading Association, 1967.

Duffy, Thomas. *Literacy Instruction in the Military.* Communication Design Center, Carnegie Mellon University, November 16, 1983.

Elligett, Jane and Thomas Tocco. "Reading Achievement in 1979 vs. Achievement in the Fifties." *Phi Delta Kappan*, June 1980.

Evans, Bertrand and James Lynch. *High School English Textbooks.* Berkeley, California: University of California, 1963.

Flesch, Rudolf. "Why Johnny Still Can't Read." *Family Circle Magazine*, November 1, 1979.

Froese, Victor. "Classics in Reading: A Survey." *The Reading Teacher*, December 1982.

Gillette, Arthur and John Ryan. "Eleven Issues in Literacy for the 1990's." *Assignment Children 63/64,* UNICEF, Geneva, Switzerland, 1983.

Groff, Patrick. "Can the Myths of Reading Instruction be Dispelled?" From Patrick Groff paper "Myths of Reading Instruction," 1983.

Gurren, Louise and Ann Hughes. "Intensive Phonics vs. Gradual Phonics in Beginning Reading: A Review." *Journal of Education Research, 58*, April 1965.

Hirsch, E.D., Jr. "Cultural Literacy." Speech, National Conference on Adult Literacy, January 20, 1984, Washington, D.C.

Hunter, Carmen St. John and David Harman. *Adult Illiteracy in the United States.* New York: McGraw-Hill, 1979.

Jacques, Joseph W. "Adult Illiteracy and Under-education in Massachusetts: Can We Afford It?" Worcester, Massachusetts: Massachusetts State College, Right to Read Academy, 1979.

Johnson, Mary. *Programmed Illiteracy in Our Schools*, Winnipeg, Canada: Clarity Books, 1971.

Komoski, Kenneth. Publishers' Responsibilities in Meeting the Continuing Challenge of Literacy. Literacy Meeting the Challenge Series. Paper presented at the National Right to Read Conference, Washington, D.C.: May 1978.

Levine, Kenneth. "Functional Literacy, Fond Illusions and False Economies." *Harvard Educational Review, 52*, No. 3, August 1982.

Mamman, Henry, Ursula Hogan, and Charles E. Greene. *Reading Instruction in the Secondary Schools*. New York: David McKay Company, Inc., 1961.

Marshall, Kim. "The Reading Problem: Some Sensible Solutions." *Learning*, April/May 1983.

Moore, Allen B. *Literacy: Meeting the Challenge*. Paper presented at National Right to Read Conference, Washington, D.C.: May 1978.

Mosse, Hilde. "Reading Disorders in the United States." *The Reading Teacher*, November 1962.

Nikifaruk, Andrew. "Why Kids Can't Read." *Quest*, September 1982.

Packard, Vance. "Are We Becoming A Nation of Illiterates? *Reader's Digest*, April 1974.

Patterson, Oliver and Lewis Pulling. "Critical Issues in Adult Illiteracy." *Outlook for the 80's*, U.S. Department of Education, Basic Skills Improvement Program, September 1981.

Pollack, Cecelia and Victor Martuza. "Teaching Reading in the Cuban Primary Schools." *The Journal of Reading, 25,* No. 3, December 1981.

Reagan, Ronald. "English of Students is a National Problem." *The Columbus Dispatch*, March 16, 1975. *Copley News Service.*

"Reporter Finds Some Surprises in Successful Reading Programs." *Education USA,* August 22, 1983.

Resnick, L.B. "Theories and Prescriptions for Early Reading Instruction." In L.B. Resnick and P.A. Weaver (Eds.) *Theory and Practice of Early Reading, 2*. Hilldales, New Jersey: Lawrence Erlbaum, 1979.

Rigg, Pat and Francis E. Kazemek. *Adult Illiteracy: Problem and Solutions.* Department of Curriculum, Instruction and Media, Southern Illinois University, Carbondale, Illinois.

Rosenblatt, Louise M. "The Acid Test for Literature Teaching." *The English Journal*, 1958.

Royster, Vermont. "The New Illiteracy." *Change*, April 1975.

Samuels, S.J. *A Discussion of the Pittsburgh Reading Conference Papers*. Paper delivered at the Conference on Theory and Practice of Beginning Reading Instruction. Pittsburgh: Pittsburgh University Learning Research and Development Center, April 1976.

Shannon, Patrick. "The Use of Commercial Reading Materials in Elementary Schools." *Reading Research Quarterly*, Fall 1983, International Reading Association.

Sheils, Merrill. "Why Johnny Can't Write." *Newsweek*, December 8, 1975.

Sticht, Thomas. *The Basic Skills Movement: Its Impact on Literacy.* Literacy: Meeting the Challenge Series. Paper presented at the National Right to Read Conference, Washington, D.C., May 1978.

Thompson, Roger. "Illiteracy in America." *Editorial Research Report, 1*, No. 24, Congressional Quarterly, Inc., June 24, 1983.

Tomorrow's Illiterates. Edited by Charles Wolcutt. Boston, Massachusetts: Little, Brown and Co., 1961.

Tractenburg, Paul. *Who is Accountable for Pupil Literacy?* Literacy: Meeting the Challenge Series. Paper presented at the National Right to Read Conference, Washington, D.C., May 1978.

Venezky, Richard. "A History of Phonics in American Reading Instruction." Conference Report. *The Reading Informer, 9*, October 1981.

Viox, Ruth C. *Evaluating Reading and Study Skills in the Secondary Classroom.* Newark, Delaware: International Reading Association, 1968.

Walcutt, C., J. Lamport, and G. McCracken. *Teaching Reading.* New York: McMillan, 1974.

Walcutt, C. "Sounding Out, No! Phonics, Yes!" *Learning, 5*, November 1976, p. 76.

Welborn, Stanley. "A Nation of Illiterates." *U.S. News and World Report*, May 17, 1982.

Yarington, David J. *The Great American Reading Machine.* Rochelle Park, New Jersey: Hayden Book, 1978.

Ziegler, Warren L. *Literacy as Self-Discovery.* International Reading Association, Symposium on New Approach to Adult Literacy, Anaheim, California: May 1976.

APPENDIX

The following is a list of effective schools programs developed by local school districts, state departments of education, and other organizations, including regional laboratories, universities, and research institutes.

The programs are organized alphabetically by state of the *developer.* Within each state, they are organized alphabetically by *name* of the developer's organization.

PROGRAM FOR EFFECTIVE TEACHING (PET)
Arkansas Department of Education, General Division
Management and Development Division
State Education Building
Little Rock, AR 72201

SCHOOL IMPROVEMENT PROGRAM (SIP)
California State Department of Education
Office of School Improvement
721 Capitol Mall
Sacramento, CA 95814

QUALITY SKILL BUILDING PROGRAM: SECONDARY LEVEL (QSB)
Los Angeles Unified School District
644 West 17th Street
Los Angeles, CA 90015

SAN DIEGO COUNTY EFFECTIVE SCHOOLS PROGRAM
San Diego County Office of Education
6401 Linda Vista Road
San Diego, CA 92111-7399

SCHOOL IMPROVEMENT THROUGH LEAGUES AND CLUSTERS
Colorado Department of Education
303 West Colfax
Denver, CO 80204

EFFECTIVE SCHOOLS PROGRAM
Mid-Continent Regional Educational Laboratory (McREL)
2600 So. Parker Road   4719 Belleview
Bldg. 5, Suite 353   Kansas City, MO 64112
Aurora, CO 80014

CONNECTICUT SCHOOL EFFECTIVENESS PROGRAM
Connecticut State Education Department
Box 2219
Hartford, CT 06115

URBAN ACADEMY PROGRAM
New Haven Board of Education
Instructional Services Center
21 Wooster Place
New Haven, CT 06511

CHICAGO EFFECTIVE SCHOOLS PROJECT (CESP)
Chicago Public Schools
Office of Equal Educational Opportunity
1819 W. Pershing Road
East Center 6
Chicago, IL 60609

SCHOOL IMPROVEMENT MODEL (SIM)
Iowa State University
College of Education
E 005 Quadrangle
Ames, IA 50011

KENTUCKY SCHOOL EFFECTIVENESS PROGRAM
Kentucky Department of Education
1810 Capital Plaza Tower
Frankfort, KY 40601

PROGRAM DEVELOPMENT EVALUATION (PDE)
Center for Social Organization of Schools
Johns Hopkins University
3505 N. Charles Street
Baltimore, MD 21218

SCHOOL IMPROVEMENT THROUGH INSTRUCTIONAL IM-PROVEMENT (SITIP)
Maryland State Department of Education (MSDE)
200 W. Baltimore Street
Baltimore, MD 21202

SCHOOL IMPROVEMENT PROGRAM
Detroit Public Schools
5057 Woodward Avenue
Detroit, MI 48202

MICHIGAN SCHOOL IMPROVEMENT PROJECT (M-SIP)
Michigan Department of Education
Box 30008
Lansing, MI 48908

PROJECT SHAL
Area 1 St. Louis School District
5234 Wells Avenue
St. Louis, MO 63113

SCHOOL IMPROVEMENT PROJECT (SIP)
New York City Board of Education
131 Livingston Street
Brooklyn, NY 11201

LOCAL SCHOOL DEVELOPMENT PROJECT (LSDP)
New York Urban Coalition
99 Hudson Street
New York, NY 10013

MIDDLE GRADES ASSESSMENT PROGRAM (MGAP)
Center for Early Adolescence
Carr Mill Mall, Suite 223
Carrboro, NC 27510

SCHOOL IMPROVEMENT IN BASIC SKILLS
Cincinnati Public Schools
230 East 9th Street
Cincinnati, OH 45202

EFFECTIVE SCHOOLS
KEDS—Kent State Center for Educational Development and
    Strategic Services
Wright Hall, Kent State University
Kent, OH 44242

EFFECTIVE SCHOOLS PROGRAM
Ohio Department of Education
65 So. Front Street
Columbus, OH 43215

**ONWARD TO EXCELLENCE/GOAL BASED EDUCATION
PROGRAM**
Northwest Regional Educational Laboratory (NWREL)
300 S.W. Sixth Avenue
Portland, OR 97204

PRINCIPALS AS INSTRUCTIONAL LEADERS
Northwest Regional Educational Laboratory (NWREL)
300 S.W. Sixth Avenue
Portland, OR 97204

SCHOOL IMPROVEMENT PROGRAM (SIP)
Pittsburgh Public Schools
West Liberty Training Center
Dunster and La Moine Streets
Pittsburgh, PA 15226

SCHOOL EFFECTIVENESS TRAINING PROGRAM
Research for Better Schools
444 North Third Street
Philadelphia, PA 19123

SCHOOL IMPROVEMENT PROCESS
South Carolina Department of Education
Office of Accreditation and Administrative Services
1429 Senate Street
Columbia, SC 29201

EFFECTIVE USE OF TIME PROGRAM
Peabody Center for Effective Teaching (PCET)
Vanderbilt University
Box 34
Nashville, TN 37203

SCHOOL EFFECTIVENESS PROGRAM
Research and Service Institute, Inc.
5126 Prince Phillip Cove
Brentwood, TN 37027

SYSTEMATIC PROGRAM FOR INSTRUCTION, REMEDIATION AND ACCELERATION OF LEARNING (SPIRAL)
Norfolk Public Schools
800 East City Hall Avenue
P.O. Box 1357
Norfolk, VA 23501

VERMONT SCHOOL IMPROVEMENT INSTITUTE
Department of Organizational Counseling and Foundational Studies
College of Education and Social Services
University of Vermont
228 Waterman Building
Burlington, VT 05405

PROJECT RISE (Rising to Individual Scholastic Excellence)
Milwaukee Public Schools
5225 West Vliet Street
P.O. Drawer 10K
Milwaukee, WI 53201

WISCONSIN PROGRAM FOR THE RENEWAL AND IMPROVE-MENT OF SECONDARY EDUCATION (WRISE)

University of Wisconsin-Madison
School of Education
1025 West Johnson Street
Madison, WI 53706

DATE DUE

AP 30 '90			
NO 20 '91			
JY 06 '92			
OCT 19 1993			
FEB 27 '96			